ISBN 978-0-484-42137-9
PIBN 10513839

E

TO

TRANSLITERATION OF HINDU AND MUHAMMADAN NAMES

IN

THE BENGAL ARMY.

PREPARED AT THE REQUEST OF THE GOVERNMENT OF INDIA,

BY

C. J. LYALL, M.A., C.I.E.,

BENGAL CIVIL SERVICE.

(THIRD EDITION.)

GUIDE

TO

THE TRANSLITERATION OF HINDU AND MUHAMMADAN NAMES

IN

THE BENGAL ARMY.

PREPARED AT THE REQUEST OF THE GOVERNMENT OF INDIA,

BY

C. J. LYALL, M.A., C.I.E.,

BENGAL CIVIL SERVICE.

Sir Charles James

(THIRD EDITION.)

CALCUTTA:

OFFICE OF THE SUPERINTENDENT OF GOVERNMENT PRINTING, INDIA.

1892.

INTRODUCTION.

Objects of this Compilation.—In 1878 the Government of India were desirous of introducing greater uniformity (as had already been done in the civil departments of the Administration) in the transliteration in official documents of the names borne by native soldiers of the Bengal Army, and the following compilation was accordingly undertaken with a view to furnish a guide in applying the principles already recognized in the official system.

Lists were made over to me containing rolls of native names in the following regiments :—

1st Native Infantry.
2nd (Prince of Wales' Own) Gurkhas
5th Native Light Infantry.
14th Sikhs.
20th Punjab Native Infantry.
23rd Pioneers.
33rd Bengal Infantry.
35th Bengal Infantry.
41st Ditto.
2nd Bengal Cavalry.
3rd Ditto.
10th Bengal Lancers.
11th Ditto.
14th Bengal Cavalry.
15th Ditto.

I subsequently received lists of names from the 43rd Assam Light Infantry; but these proved to be so indistinctly and irregularly written, and to contain so many names of *Jharuwas* (Meches, Rábbas, and others from Goálpára), *Kachāris* (from Kámrúp and Darrang), *Manipuris*, and other natives of Assam which I was at the time unable to fix with certainty, that I was obliged to exclude them from the compilation. From the lists of the remaining fifteen regiments the following pages have been compiled.

2. **Materials of the Compilation.**—The lists supplied to me vary much in copiousness. For some regiments (notably the 2nd Gurkhas) only a few selected names have

been given; for others apparently almost the whole muster-roll has been copied out. In some lists the castes, as well as the personal names, have been supplied; in others not. The names have been written in the vernacular only by the regimental munshis, and there has been much discrepancy in spelling. In reproducing them here, I have thought it best generally to accept the spellings as I found them. In some cases these peculiar spellings represent local varieties of pronunciation (*e.g.* in Dogra names in the list of the 20th Native Infantry there is a constant recurrence of a doubled consonant after a long vowel, as Bhollu, Suchetta, Rasílla, &c., which is contrary to the rule prevailing in most parts of Hindustan): in some they represent a more genuine vernacular than the more literary and usual spellings (*e.g.* Siu सिउ is a better representation of the sound heard, and follows more closely the laws which change Sanskrit words into Prákrit, than the commoner Shiv or Shiu शिव); but in the majority of instances the difference is simply one of greater or less conformity to the Sanskrit original. There is a constant tendency on the part of Hindu scribes to revert to the original type, in spite of the fact that the person to whom the name belongs uses it in its vernacular form both in speaking and writing. Thus, a man may call himself Kisun or Kishan, but the regimental pandit will write him down Ḳrishn; he may call himself Lachhman or Lakkhan, but appear in the list as Lakshman; and so on. Between the strict Sanskrit form and the exact reproduction of the modern vernacular the gradations are numerous, and it is impossible to say without hearing a man pronounce his own name how far he has accommodated himself, or has been accommodated by the pandit, to the classical standard.

Nevertheless, perhaps because these lists are for the most part made for practical use, and the men are actually called every day by their names as entered in them, they exhibit less pedantry than might be expected ; and, as a collection of genuine Hindu and Musalmán names, drawn from the Punjab, the North-Western Provinces, Oudh, Bihar, Rajputana, the Himalayan districts, and the Trans-Indus tracts, they are of considerable interest and value. They are far from being exhaustive ; any one familiar with the people who reads through the names under a single letter will readily supply perhaps as many more as are contained in this compilation ; but for our present purpose of showing how such names may be uniformly spelt, and elucidating the principles on which they are formed, they are sufficient.

3. **Rules for transliteration.**—The system of transliteration adopted is that prescribed by the Government of India. The following table shows the equivalent English, Devanágari, and Persian letters :—

VOWELS.

Devanágari.	*Persian.*	*English.*
अ	اَ	a
आ	آ	á
इ	اِ	i
ई	اِي	í
उ	اُ	u
ऊ	اُو	ú
ऋ	رِ	ri
ए	اے	e
ऐ	اَي	ai
ओ	او	o
औ	اَو	au

CONSONANTS.

क	ک	k
ख	کھ	kh
—	خ	kh
—	ق	k

Consonants—*continued.*

Devanágari.	*Persian.*	*English.*
ग	گ	g
घ	گھ	gh
—	غ	gh
च	چ	ch
छ	چھ	chh
ज	ج	j
ज़	ظ ض ذ ز	z
झ	جھ	jh
—	ژ	zh
ट	ٹ or ٿ	ṭ
ठ	ٹھ or ٿھ	ṭh
ड	ڈ or ڐ	ḍ
ढ	ڈھ or ڐھ	ḍh
ड़	ڑ or ڙ	ṛ
ढ़	ڑھ or ڙھ	ṛh
ण	ن	n
त	ت ط	t
थ	تھ	th
द	د	d
ध	دھ	dh
न	ن	n
प	پ	p
फ	پھ	ph
फ़	ف	f
ब	ب	b
भ	بھ	bh
म	م	m
य	ي	y
र	ر	r
ल	ل	l
व	و	v *or* w*

* The *v* sound of this letter is in Hindustan usually replaced by ब *b*. When intended to be pronounced as *w* it commonly receives a dot underneath, व़

Consonants—*continued*.

Devanágari.	*Persian.*	*English.*
श	ش	sh
ष	کھ ش	sh (*more usually* kh)
स	ص ، س ، ث	s
ह	ح ، ہ	h
ं & ँ	ں	n̲
—	ع	ʼ

In using the above table for the conversion of vernacular names into the Roman character, the following points should be borne in mind :—

4. Rules for use of accents.—The long are distinguished from the short vowels by the acute accent. This expedient has two defects: (1) it prohibits the employment of this diacritical mark for the purpose of indicating the tonic accent of the word, which frequently does not fall on the syllable in which a long vowel occurs; and (2) it is a difficulty to writers and printers, who are apt to forget the necessity of marking a long vowel with an accent. To obviate the first, it is desirable to restrict as far as possible the application of the accent to those syllables which are not only long but also bear the tonic accent; and to obviate the second, the use of the accent should be as sparingly resorted to as is consistent with the due pronunciation of the word.

It is very rarely necessary to mark a vowel long when it ends a word in an open syllable; this is because in such a position it seldom bears the tonic accent, and because it is also, in the form of Hindi to which these names belong, in such a position *always long*. Short terminal vowels have in the modern language ceased to be pronounced, and therefore such names as Indar-man, Lachhmi-pat, though often pedantically written इंद्रमणि, लक्ष्मी पति, should not be read as of four, but as of three syllables. The only exception where it is necessary to mark terminal vowels as long is when such a vowel forms an imperfect diphthong with a preceding short vowel, as in the names Meraí मेड़ई, Mataú, मतऊ. In this position it receives the tonic accent, and as the combination has a different sound from the pure diphthong *ai* or *au*, it is useful to mark the distinction graphically.

In a *closed* syllable at the end of a word, whether the letter following the long vowel be a complete consonant or *anunásika*, the vowel should be marked by an accent, as in such positions it ordinarily receives the tonic accent.

When, in a compound name, the first element ends in a long vowel which, if the first element stood alone, would not be accented, the accent in the compound falls (in the absence of *sandhi*, or fusion) on the same syllable as would receive it if the words stood apart; and therefore in these cases also it is not necessary to mark the vowel long. Thus, गङ्गा, देबी, सर्जू, standing alone, would be written Ganga, Debi, Sarju, not Gangá, Debí, Sarjú: aud the compound names Ganga-dhar, Debi-dín, Sarju-parshád need not therefore receive an accent on the second syllable, as in them also it does not receive any tonic accent.

The same principle may be applied to many compounds, even in cases of *sandhi*: thus, महाराज may be written Maharáj, महानन्द Mahanand, रामानन्द Rámanand, because the long middle syllable does not bear the tonic accent, which falls in all three cases on the last syllable. In the mouths of the people an unaccented long vowel constantly tends to become short. Thus, महराज is the ordinary pronunciation of महाराज; नारायण is most frequently नरायन; दामोदर appears in the list as दमोदर. This justifies us in omitting the accent over a long vowel when it does not receive a special stress in utterance.

Note that *e* and *o* are, after long vowels, regularly expressed by य and व: *e.g.* Sabáe is written सहाय, Ráe राय, Deo देव.

5. Diacritical marks for Consonants.—In transliterating the consonants, it is important to mark in writing the distinction between the cerebral and non-cerebral letters, between the káf ق and simple k ک, and between the *anunásika* and the perfect nasal, as these are differences which very materially affect the pronunciation In *printed* notifications, in which the dotted letters may perhaps cause inconvenience, the distinction is not so essential. It is needless to mark the distinction between the nasals of the *k*, *ch*, *ṭ*, and *t* series, as their place sufficiently indicates their sounds.

Note that it is a common device in Panjábi names to indicate a doubled nasal by prefixing *anunásika* to a single perfect nasal. Thus, *Chunni* is written चुंनी, *Naránne* नरांने, etc. The sign *anuswára* (ं) is that now employed almost universally for *anunásika* (ँ), as well as for the prefixed nasals of the five organs. It has its original sound only when it precedes ह (where it sounds as *ng*, with an audible *g*, and is often so written) and स, (where it is a less forcible *ng*, but still different from the soft nasal *anunásika**). The *anunásika* is often inserted in an apparently arbitrary manner in names where it had originally no place: thus, लछमीं *Lachhmíṇ* is common for लच्छमी, भैरों *Bhairoṇ* for भैरव, कांसी *Káṇsi* for काशी; but the sound is very soft, and the names are also commonly found without it. It would conduce to uniformity if it were in such cases omitted in transliteration.

6. Rules for Arabic names.—Arabic names (such as are most of those proper to Musalmáns) are in India invariably pronounced, not as they sound in Arabic, but as they were pronounced in the Turáni Persian from which the Indian vernaculars have been recruited. The proper sounds of ث and ص have been lost; ح is uttered like ه; ز, ذ, ض and ظ are all like the English *z*. ط, though it is nearer the cerebral ट than the dental त, is pronounced like the latter. خ and غ, being letters found in Persian, as well as Arabic words, have kept better their original sounds, though the vulgar generally

---

* Compare the difference in sound between सिंह (anuswára) and मुँह and मेँह (anunásika); and between हंसो (anuswára) and हँसना (anunásika).

pronounce the former like *k* क (*not kh* ख) and the latter like *g* ग (*not gh* घ). The syllable بخش is invariably in Hindu names pronounced (as a dissyllable) as if it were written बकस ; بخشش appears in Tulsi-dás's *Rámayan* (and is heard every day in the vernacular) as बकसीस ; غلام is गुलाम and تيغ तेग. As, however, the correct pronunciation of these two letters has the preponderance of authority and is generally understood, it is better to use it for transliteration. The correct sound of the ق is also (this being a favourite Turki letter and thus common with people of that race in India) not seldom heard ; the speakers of Hindí render it by simple क, or sometimes by ख (as वख़त for وقت). Another Arabic letter the correct sound of which is occasionally attempted is ع; but it is usually inaudible before a vowel, while after one it either prolongs the vowel sound (جعفر, *Ja'far*, sounding as *Jáfar*, يعقوب *Ya'kúb* as *Yákúb*), or adds a syllable to the word (نعمت, *Ni'mat*, ordinarily *Niamat* or even *Niámat*).

Among the special peculiarities of the Indian pronunciation of Arabic names are the conversion of *ai* to *e* (شيخ, *Shekh*, properly *Shaikh*, حسين *Husen*, properly *Husain*, سليمان *Sulemán*, properly *Sulaimán*, ايمن *Eman*, properly *Aiman*), and the insertion of the vowel *e* between final ح and a preceding consonant (فتح, invariably *Fateh*, in Hindi फत्ते, properly *Fatḥ*, صبح *subeh*, for *subḥ*).

I.—How Hindu names are formed.

7. Classes of names among Hindus.—Hindu names may be broadly divided into (1) the religious and (2) the non-religious or secular. Religious names are those which are either the names or attributes of deities or holy personages or places, or express some kind of relation to them. Non-religious names may be either those of legendary or historical personages of former times; or descriptive, taken from some peculiarity of appearance or personal incident ; or martial, expressive of valour; or (a very numerous class) depreciatory names designed to avert the evil eye. All names may appear either in their primitive form or as diminutives; they may be either simple or compound.

8. Names preferred by special castes and races.—Particular classes display a preference for particular kinds of names. Thus, Brahmans more commonly have religious names, and especially names referring to Shiva or Mahadeo, than other castes; Sikhs and Rajputs always append सिंह to their personal names, and while the former are fond of titles describing martial exploits or places where battles were fought (Panjáb Singh, Multán Singh, Kábul Singh, &c.), and of the names of their Gurus (Nának, Angad, Lehna), the latter commonly use the names or attributes of deities or famous heroes of old. Gurkhas prefer martial names of a peculiar type, in which compounds are often formed of Hindí and Persian (Mast-bír, Jang-bír, Ran-bahádur, &c.). Játs and Gújars are fond of familiar names, especially those designed to avert the evil eye.

9. Hindu names borrowed from Persian.—A good many Hindu names are borrowed from the Persian;* the following are examples chosen from the first few letters of the alphabet:—

Ajab .	عجب
Ajáib .	عجائب
Akbar .	اکبر
Álam .	عالم
Amán .	امان
Amír .	امیر
Árámi .	آرامی
Ashrafi .	اشرفی
Bádám .	بادام
Bahádur .	بهادر
Bahál .	بحال
Bakhshish.	بخشش
Bakht .	بخت
Bakhtáwar	بختاور
Baland .	بلند
Barkat .	برکت
Báz .	باز
Beg	بیگ
Bunyád .	بنیاد
Chaman .	چمن
Dariáo .	دریا
Daulat .	دولت
Díwán .	دیوان
Díwána .	دیوانه

and all those beginning with F.

* Persian includes Arabic. No Arabic words have come into Hindustani except through Persian.

Many Hindí names are of mixed origin, Persian elements having been adapted to Hindí modes of composition, or Hindí elements having been brought into Persian forms. Of the former the following are examples:—

Chit-bahál ("one who has presence of mind"),	. . .	from	चित + بحال
Dil-pat ("Lord of the heart"),		,,	دل + पति
Dil-sukh ("delight of the heart"),		,,	دل + सुख
Garíb-Rám ("the poor on whom Rám has mercy"),	. .	,,	غريب + राम
Gauhar-chand,	. . .	,,	گوهر + चंद
Gulzárı-Lál,	. . .	,,	گلزار + लाल
Jimi-pál,	. . . .	,,	زمين + पाल

Of the latter the commonest type is that formed of *bakhsh* (root of بخشيدن) with the name of a deity, meaning "the gift of ———"; others are such names as Ran-bahádur, Jang-bír, &c.

The majority of Hindu names are, however, of native, not of foreign origin; and before endeavouring to classify them as to meaning and source, it is necessary to consider the forms which they take. They are either single words or compounds, either in their original shape or diminutives.

10. Hindi compounds.—The single words and the compounds may be either religious or secular: the first may be names of deities, demi-gods, heroes, holy places, holy men, sacred rivers or mountains, or may be adjectives or nouns, originally perhaps descriptions or attributes of some person or place belonging to the first category. The compounds are, however, the more ordinary form in which the names of deities or other sacred objects are exhibited; and perhaps it is generally with an understood, if not expressed supplement, such as is found in the compounds, that the single names are used. When a man styles himself Bhagwán, or Bishan, or Bihári, he is not to be taken as identifying himself with Vishnu the preserver, but rather as expressing his trust in that particular god; his idea is the same as is explicitly conveyed when he uses a compound form,—Bhagwán-dín "the submissive to Vishnu," Bishan-dayál "Vishnu is merciful," Bihári-dás "the servant of Krishna." *

Compound names are either such as are taken, already compounded, straight out of Sanskrit, as Manohar "the mind-ravishing," Gopál "the cowherd," Dámodar "secured by a cord round the middle," Girdhári "the mountain upholder," Chaturbhuj "the four-armed"; or are formed of elements still separately recognizable in Hindí, but put together upon the patterns of that ancient language from which Hindí draws its stores. They may generally be described in the terms of Sanskrit grammar, even when the elements are distinctly Hindí Thus, to illustrate the practice from the large number of compounds in the following pages of which Rám forms the first member, Rám-adhín "subject to Rám," is a *tat-purusha*, or dependent compound; so also are Rám-autár "the incarnation of Rám," Rám-charan "the feet of Rám," Rám-dín "the submissive to Rám," Rám-parshád "the grace of Rám," Rám-charitr "the deeds of Rám," Rám-kírat "the fame of Rám," &c.

Rám-anand "he whose delight is Rám," Rám-baran "he whose caste (or colour) is that of Rám," Rám-bharos "he whose hope is Rám," Rám-basáwan "he who has Rám to establish him," Rám-jiáwan "he whose life-giver is Rám," Rám-lochan "he whose eye is Rám," &c., are *bahu-vríhi*, or relative compounds.

Ram-Gopál, "Rám and Gopál," "Rám-Kisun, "Rám and Krishna," Rati-Rám, "Rám and Rati," Rádha-Kishan,

---

* This is implied by the frequent rejection in common speech of the subordinate member in a compound name: thus Tulsi-dás, the poet, is familiarly spoken of as Tulsi, Námdeo as Náma, &c.

" Rádha and Krishna," Richa-Rám,* "the Vedic songs and Rám," are *dwandwa*, or aggregative compounds.

Anant Rám "the eternal Rám," Akbe Rám "the imperishable Rám," Abináshi Rám "the undying Rám," Átma Rám" "Rám, the soul of all things," Sat Rám "the true Rám," and the host of names ending in Lál ("child," "darling" *i.e.* the infant Krishna) preceded by an adjective (*e.g.* Bihári "sportive," Achchhe "good," Pyáre "dear," Shám "dark-skinned," &c.) or a noun used adjectively (*e.g.* Makkhan "butter," referring to one of the child Krishna's exploits related in the Prem Ságar, Nand, the name of Krishna's foster-father, Sukh "delight," &c.) are all *karma-dháraya*, or descriptive compounds.

But, besides these compounds, the parts of the first three of which, since they form one composite word, should be united by a hyphen, there are other compound names which may be regarded as short sentences with the substantive verb left out, *e.g.* Ganga-dayál "the Ganges (is) merciful," Suphal Rám "Rám is fruitful," Sada Rám† "Ram is eternal," Sahaj Rám "gentle is Rám." These may be written either with or without a hyphen.

The above cases (including the extremely common class of names in *bakhsh* already mentioned, of which the type is borrowed from the Persian) will be found to comprise the vast majority of Hindu compound names. When the parts of a compound can easily be separated, it is best to write them separately, either with or without a hyphen (but capital letters should not be used for a subordinate element unless it is a proper name), both because their meaning is thus made clearer, and because, in the absence of *sandhi*, as already noticed, the tonic accent falls on that syllable in each element on which it would fall if it were a separate word.

---

* Probably this is the correct form of the name given in the lists as रिछाराम.

† Perhaps this name is formed on a false analogy, to correspond with Sada-shiva Sadashiu), which, however, does not mean the "eternal Shiva," but "the ever happy." Such false analogies are very common.

11. Diminutives.—Names are constantly found in a diminutive or familiar form, and some notice is necessary of the changes which they undergo under these circumstances. The usual process is to shorten a long vowel, to double a consonant, and to add a termination, either *á*, *í*, or *ú* (most commonly the last). Thus, Rám becomes Rammu; Lál, Lallu; Bhím, Bhimma; Rádha, Raddhu; Sib, Sibhu; Nának, Nanku; Mangal, Mangali and Mangalu; Kán, Kannu; Káli, Kallu. Another favourite termination is *aí* (अई), as in Kánh, Kanhaí; Sukh, Sukhaí; Budh, Budhaí. In these cases the shifting of the accent prohibits the doubling of the consonant preceding the termination. If the original word be a compound or long, only the first part of it is taken and the rest rejected *e.g.* Ghan-shám, Ghanaí; Dalpat, Dallu; Paras-Ram, Parsu; Pitambar, Pitaí; Sobha Rám, Subhaí. Diminutives ending in *í*, *ú*, and *aí* are further developed by the addition of another syllable, *a*, thus: Lál, Lallu, Lalluwa or Lalwa; Dhan, Dhaní, Dhaniya; Ghan-shám, Ghanaí, Ghanaiya; Kánh, Kanhaya; Natthu, Natthuwa; Ganga, Gangu, Gangua.

Many names present an oblique form in *e*, instead of the nominative in *a*: *e.g.* Bhagole, Bhúre, Chhabíle, Gaje, Karore, Kuṛe, Máṇḍe, Máṛe, Matole, Nanhe, Pyáre, Rádhe, Ráje, Sáṇge. Perhaps this is because they are in the vocative case; or it may be due to contraction of the diminutive ending *aí*; or in compounds (Rádhe Kishn, Ráje Rám, although Rádha and Rája are both words which do not ordinarily suffer inflection) it may be caused by an obscure sense that in construction, final *á* requires to be changed to *e*, just as *hissadár* is ordinarily pronounced *hissedar*.

12. Sources of Religious names: Deities.—It remains to give some examples of the different classes of objects chosen as religious names. Among deities, Vishnu, in his alternative names of Náráyan, Bhagwán and Hari, and in his incarnations as Ráma and Krishna, stands by far at the head of name-givers; other incarnations contained in the list are Paras Rám (Parasuráma), Narsingh (Nara-singha), and Sáligrám (frequently, but wrongly, supposed to be divisible into Sálig and Rám, and as such yielding Sálik, Sálag, Salku, &c.) Ráma has few alternative names, Krishna an immense number, for the most part drawn from the history of his childhood, as related in the Bhágavata Purána. The Hindí translation of the 10th chapter of this work, known as the Prem Ságar, is full of passages throwing light on common Hindu names which might otherwise be obscure. Among the commonest Krishna-names are the following:—

Bál Gopál ("the child-cowherd")
Bál-mukund ("the mighty child").
Bansi-dhar ("the flute-holder").
Básdeo ("the son of Vasudeva").
Bihári ("the sportive").
Bishnáth ("the Lord of all")
Dámodar ("tied by a string round the middle").
Ghan-shám ("dark-skinned, like the colour of clouds").
Girdhar, Girdhári, ("mountain-holder").
Gobind (probably "Lord of kine").
Gopál ("cowherd").
Gopi-náth ("Lord of the Gopis or Milkmaids of Braj").
Jagan-náth ("Lord of the world").
Kánh (the Prákrit-Hindi form of the Sanskrit Krishna).
Kesab, Keso ("the long-haired").
Kunj-bihári, ("he who sports in the thickets").
Líla-dhar ("the playful").
Mádho ("the slayer of Madhu").
Makkhan-chor ("the butter thief").
Man-mohan ("the bewitcher of the soul").
Manohar ("the charming").
Mohan ("the charming").
Murári ("the foe of Mura").
Murli-dhar ("the flute-player").
Nand-kishor ("Nanda's boy").
Nand-kumár ("Nanda's prince").
Prabhu ("the Lord").
Rádha-ballabh ("the lover of Radha")

Sáṉwal (" the dark-complexioned ").
Shám (" the dark-complexioned ").

Other personages belonging to the Krishna-legend whose names are common are—

Balarám (Baldeo), his brother.
Nand, his foster-father.
Jasoda, his foster-mother.
Basdeo, his father.
Deoki, his mother.
Rádhika, Rádha, his mistress (surnamed Lalita "the eager," which appears in the list as Lálta).
Udho, a friend and follower.

Krishna and Balarám are often joined in the name Jugal-kishor "the pair of lads"

Rám (Rám-Chandar) has only the following few alternative names in common use:—

Raghu-bar,— (" the best,— ⎫
Raghu-náth,—(" the Lord,— ⎪
Raghu-bír,— (" the hero,— ⎬ of Raghu's race "
Raghu-pat,— (" the Lord,— ⎪
Raghu-nandan,—" the darling,— ⎭

His brothers Bharat and Lachhman, his monkey-helpers Hanumán and Sugríb, and his wife Síta (Jánuki, Jánki), are the chief characters of his legend which have supplied popular names.

It should be noted that *Náth* (" Lord ") commonly indicates Visnnu among the Gods, while *Ísar* (Íshwar) is the termination proper to Shiva or Mahadeo, his great rival.

The latter, with his consort Bhawáni (synonyms Káli, Chandi, Gauri, Debi, Durga, Párbati, Tára, Kámta, Uma, and Máta " the mother ") has produced a very large number of names. The alternative names of Shiva are—

Bhairo (" the terrible ").
Bisesar (Visweswara " Lord of all ").
Bhola-náth (" husband of Bhola or Párbati ").
Ganga-dhar (" the upholder of the Ganges ").

Har (final short vowels having disappeared, this word stands for Hara, Shiva, as well as Hari, Vishnu. The two are conjoined in Hari-Har).

Mahes, Mahesar } "Great Lord."
Paramesar, "The supreme Lord."
Rudr, Rudar.
Sankar, Shankar, "bringer of good luck."

The names compounded with Shiu (Siu) rival in number those which contain Rám.

Benares (Kási) is the great centre of Shiva-worship, and names having reference to this god are most frequent in the districts adjoining that city and in Oudh.

Other gods and goddesses whose names will be found in the lists annexed are—

Brahm (in the single name Brahm-dayál).
Indar.
Lachhmi or Lakhmí (wife of Vishnu, and also called Srí).
Ganes or Gan-pat also called (Gaj-ráj, "the elephant king").
Rati, "the Goddess of love"
Súraj, Súr, Ádit, "the sun."
Chandar, Chánd, Chand, "the moon" (for which the Persian Máhtáb is common).
Mangal, "the planet Mars."
Budh, "the planet Mercury."
Som "the Soma plant" (also used for "the Moon").
Tulsi, "the holy basil" (also called Brinda, Binda).

Of these the most popular are Súraj ,"the Sun," and Chand "the Moon." The latter is very commonly used as a second element in names like Amír-chand, Fakír-chand, Gauhar-chand, &c., where it is difficult to assign to it any specific sense.

13. Adjectives having reference to deities.—Besides these direct names of deities, the list abounds in adjectives which must be understood to have reference to some divine name which is not expressed. Such words are—

Achal, "the immovable."	Bichitr, "the Diverse."
Ajít, "the unconquerable."	Bijai, Bije, "the Victorious."
Akhe, "the imperishable."	Dáta, "the Giver."　.
Amar, "the immortal."	Dayál, "the compassionate."
Anant, "the endless."	Jiwrákhan, "the life-preserver."
Anek, "the manifold."	Jiáwan, Jíwan, "the life-giver."
Anúp, "the incomparable."	Kirpál, "the merciful."
Atráj, "the great king."	Maha, 'the Great."
Bhúp, Bhúpál, "the Protector of the Earth."	Pál, "the protector."
	Saháe, "the helper."

14. Names derived from holy places.—Holy places —cities, rivers, mountains, and places of pilgrimage—supply many names. Such are—

Cities.

Ayodhya (Ajudhya, Ajodhya),	Gobardhan, Gordhan.
Bindraban (*corrupt for* Brinda-ban).	Gokul.
	Kási.
Dwárika, Dwárka.	Mathura.
Gaya.	Prayág, Prág.

Rivers.

Ganga	Sarju.
Jamuna, Jamna.	

Mountains.

Himanchal.	Sumer.
Kailás.	

Places of Pilgrimage.

Hardwár.	Baijnáth.
Tribeni.	

15. Miscellaneous religious names.—Among miscellaneous religious names may be mentioned those derived from the Scripture: Bed, Achhar, Bachan, Granthi, Sáhib (Sáheb). The last is the name by which the Granth, or sacred volume, is known among the Sikhs; those of the Sikh Gurus and other religious teachers—Nának, Angad (Lahna, or Lehna, which was his name before he became Guru), Arjun, Malúk, Jaideo, Kabír, and the names beginning with Gur (for Guru); and words expressive of faith or devotion, such as Ása "hope," Bhagat "worshipper," Prem "love," Sukh "peace," Chain "rest," Sewak "servant," Sewa "service," &c.

16. Non-religious names.—The non-religious class of names are derived from very various sources. Only the main divisions can here be indicated, since many names which probably belong to this class have not yet been satisfactorily explained:—

I.—Names of Heroes.

Álha, Āla.
Ahibaran.
Arjun.
Bairisál.
Bhíkham.
Bhím.
Bhoj.
Bikramajít, Bikram.
Chhatarsál.
Chandarbhán.
Dalíp.
Hamír.

II.—Martial names.

Bágh, "tiger."
Bahádur, "valiant."
Bali, Balwant "mighty."
Bír "hero"
Bír-bal "with the might of a hero."
Dal-jít, "vanquisher of armies."
Dal-pat, "Lord of armies."
Dal-thamban "withstander of hosts"
Dhíraj, "firmness."
Durjan, "enemy."
Fatte, "victory."
Faujdár, "General."
Hákim, "Commander."
Hazári, "Captain of a thousand."
Himmat, "valour."
Hukam, "command."
Jabbár, "mighty"
Jahángír, "world conqueror")
Jai, "victory"
Jangi, "warlike."
Jaswant "famous."
Jhanda, "banner."
Jodh, "battle."
Kesri, Kehari, "lion."
Kharag, Khalak, Kharga, Kharku, "sword."
Máhma for Mahima, "greatness"
Maharáj, "Great King."
Mall, "warrior," "wrestler."
Mastán, "intoxicated," *i.e.*, with warlike fury.
Matwála, "intoxicated."

Muhkam, "strong."
Náhar, "tiger."
Nirbho, "fearless."
Pahár, "mountani."
Pahlwán "warrior".
Paltan, "battalion."
Rajiwant, Rajwant, Rájmán, "regiment."
Ran, "battle."
Ran-bír, "hero in battle."
Ran-dhír, "firm in battle."
Ran-jor, "joiner of battle."
Risál, "troop."
Sajáda, Sháh-záda, "prince."
Sámant, Sanwant, "champion."
Sangrám, "battle."
Sardár, "Captain"
Shamsher, "sword."
Sher, "lion."
Singh, "lion."
Tej, "glory."
Tek, "support".
Ujágar, "famous."
Ujjal. "glorious."
Umráo, "princely."
Wazír, "minister"
Záhir, "conspicuous."
Zálim, overbearing."
Zoráwar, "mighty."

III.—Names derived from some personal quality, physical or moral.

Achának. "sudden."
Aindha, "one who struts or walks in an absurd manner."
Albel, Arbel, "fop"
Bánka, "dandy."
Bhuj-bal, "strong-armed."
Bhúra, "brown."
Budh, &c., "old."
Budh, &c., "wise."
Chhabíla "handsome."
Chhail, top or dandy."
Chatur, Chokha, "clever."
Chaukas, "cautious."
Chiranji, Chiranju, "long-lived."
Chhote, "little."
Dhaula "white."
Dhauntál,' rich, strong, wicked."
Dhera, "squint-eyed."
Dinga, "boaster."
Ghamanda, "arrogant."
Julphi (Zulfi), "long-locked."
Kála, "black."
Khúbi, "beauty."
Khushi, "gladness."
*Khushhál, &c, "prosperous,"
Mihrbán, "friendly."
Mít, Mit, "friend."
Mitthu (diminutive), "sweet."
Muláim, "gentle."
Nadán, "foolish,"
Nanhe, "puny."
Rasíla, 'voluptuous."
Sádhu, "pious."
Sant, "mild."
Sánwal, "dark-complexioned."
Shitáb, "quick."
Taríf (تعريف, "praise," "excellent."
Tunde "one born without hands."
Turti, Turanti, "quickness."

* This word has, as will be seen from the list under K, a great many diffe ent graphic forms. Its great popularity as a name probably arises from its likeness to the Hind कुसल (कुशल) Which also appears in the list and has the sam meaning.

IV.—Depreciatory names, given to avert a Nemesis or the evil eye.

These generally name the person after somcthing mean, disgusting, trivial, or of little value, and are extremely common, especially among the agricultural castes The following are found in the lists :—

Chenchu, Chenchlu, (from *chench*), "a noxious weed."
Chhadámi "worth only six *dáms*, or a quarter of a pice."
Chhāju, Chhájja, Chhajju, (from *chháj*), "a winnowing basket."
Chhaṭṭu (from *chhatna*), "a sieve for separating the husk from grain."
Chhedi, Chhedu, (from *chheda*), a borer or weevil.
Chhíṭan, "a crumb".
Chhítar, "an old shoe."
Chuhaṛ, Chúhaṛ, "a sweeper, scavenger."
Ḍalaí, from *dala*, "a clod."
Ḍál, "a branch."
Ḍaru, "a cowardly knave."
Ḍhela, "a clod."
Ganḍa, "four *kauṛis*" (a packet of four kauris used, attached to an infant's neck, as a talisman to avert the evil eye).
Gaun, "a grain-sack."
Ghasíṭa, "dragged along the ground."
Ghisaí, Ghísan, Ghisiáwan, Ghísu, (from *ghisa*), "rubbed," "worn out."
Ghethal, "a shoe "
Ghoṭa, "a rubber for polishing"
Ghúru, (from *ghúra*), "sweepings of a dunghill."
Gudaṛ, "a ragged quilt."
Jhabba, "a leathern measure for oil."
Jhám, "a large hoe."
Jháu, "a tamarisk-bush, used for brooms."
Kauṛu, Kauṛa, "from *kauṛi*"
Kiḍḍa, Kíṛi, "a worm or insect."
Kuṛa }
Kuṛe } "sweepings."
Kúṛhe }
Máre, "mean."
Nathu, Natthu, Natthuwa, "If a man has lost several male children, the nose of the next-born is pierced, and a

nose-ring (*nath*) inserted in order that he may be mistaken for a girl, and so passed over by the evil spirits". —(*J. M. Douie in "Panjab Notes and Queries," December, 1883, page 26.*)

Phál, "ploughshare."
Phangan, from *phanga*, "grasshopper."
Phíku, from *phíka*, "tasteless"
Phen̠kún̠, *phen̠kna*, "to throw away."
Roṛa, Rúṛa, "a brickbat."
Ruldu, "a vagabond."
Sohan, "a file."

These names are ordinarily given to children born after previous children have died, in consequence, as the parents suppose, of the envy or malice of some god or demon, and the idea is that children called by such unworthy names will be passed over in future.

Besides these four main classes, the list contains many names of a miscellaneous character, most of which are easily intelligible with the help of a dictionary, while of several I can at present offer no explanation. Many are familiar or pet names, as Barkat "blessing," Bháu "brother," Bhíkha "boon," "alms," Chúṛ "top knot," Dulár (Dulál) "darling," Guláb "rose," Med, Umed, "hope," &c. Some indicate the asterism under which a child was born, as Baisákha, Bhadaí, Chaitu, Múl, Púsu, Sáwan. In fact, it is difficult to suggest the circumstances which may *not* give occasion for a household name. Of unfavourable nicknames the lists contain hardly any examples, though the class is numerous; people do not usually call themselves by the ridiculous or offensive names which the wit of their friends may invent for them, and these lists of course show only the names which the bearers of them themselves approve.

III.—MUHAMMADAN NAMES.

17. General remarks.—No such variety of form and spelling as is found in the case of Hindu names exists in those of Musalmáns. The vast majority of the latter are of Arabic origin, and their spelling and pronunciation are definitely fixed by the grammatical rules of the language to wich they belong. The cases in which the original form has been corrupted in India are few; and the list of names which are of purely Indian derivation and not controlled by the strict rules of Arabic and Persian etymology is small.

18. Orthography.—In regard to orthography, the following points deserve notice:—

(1) A vast number of names contain the Arabic article *al* ال, the vowel of which, when preceded by another vowel, is replaced by the latter. Thus, in the name 'Abdul Ghafúr, the *u* which precedes the *l* is the terminal vowel of the word *'abdu*, and it is therefore wrong to write the name, as is ordinarily done, 'Abd-ul-Ghafúr. The strict orthography would be 'Abdu-l-Ghafúr, or 'Abdu'l-Ghafúr; but for practical purposes it is sufficient to use one hyphen, after the article and before the significant noun. The same rule applies to names compounded with *Dín*, as Badrud-dín, 'Aláud-dín, Baháud-dín.

(2) There is one word of which the article *al* forms a part in which the fusion of syllables is so complete that no hyphen is needed. This is *Allah*, "God." In Persian and Hindustani the last syllable of this name, which is long by nature, is ordinarily pronounced as it it were short. The word stands for *al-Iláh*; but the *i* has been lost, and the *l* of the article coalesces with that of the noun, the accent being transferred (unlike the case of other nouns with the prefixed article) to the penultimate. No advantage would be gained by writing the name Habíbullah, according to the strictly grammatical division of its parts, Habíbu-l-lah; and to do so would tend to cause the verbal

accent, which falls on the penultimate, to be wrongly placed. In the case of such names, therefore, no hyphen is used. It would be wrong, for the reason stated above under (1), to divide them, as is sometimes done, thus—Habíb-ul-lah, Ináyat Ullah, &c.

(3) The name *Allah* (originally *Alláh*) is subjected to further abbreviation when it forms the first member of a Persian or Hindi compound, and appears as *Alah* (Alah-bakhsh, Alah-rakkha, Alah-ditta, Alah-yár). The list contains two names (Ilah-bakhsh, Ilah-dád) in which, instead of *Allah* the indefinite *Ilah* (without the prefixed *al*) is used. Another example is the name Iláh-ábád (*vulgarly* Allahabad, *Hindi* I'lah-bás). In these the article is dropped because the compound is Persian, in which language there is no article, although in common parlance *Allah* retains it. Where a pronoun is affixed to *Allah*, or an adjective formed from it, the article is, according to the rules of Arabic grammar, regularly dropped. "My God" is *Iláhi*; the same word signifies "divine."

(4) The izáfat is hardly ever used in Persian compounds except in the name Banda-e'Ali (often pronounced Bande-'Ali), and perhaps one or two other rare cases (the only examples contained in the list are 'Atá-e Muhammad, Khán-i Zamán, and Yad-i A'zam). Properly speaking, the izáfat is required in all such names as Altáf Husain, Amán 'Ali, 'Atá Husain, Aulád 'Ali, &c., where two nouns, not constructed with the Arabic article, occur in a possessive relation one to the other; but in such names it is seldom or never heard in India.

(5) It is a peculiarity of Panjábi Musalmán names that the Arabic article is suppressed before the word *Dín* "religion." Thus, the name elsewhere fully rendered Badrud-dín is in the Panjáb Badr-dín: other examples in the list are Burhán-dín, Fateh-dín, Kamál-dín, Mihráb-dín, Muhammad-dín, Muhkam-dín, Sadr-dín, Sáhib-dín, Shams-dín. In Alah-dín and Muhammad-dín, and possibly in Sáhib-dín, the second element may perhaps be the Hindi word *dín*, "subject," "submissive."

(6) There are some peculiarities in the Indian pronunciation of Arabic names, most of which have been noticed in footnotes to the list. Double letters are reduced to single ones in Hak for Hakk, Háji for Hájji, Hub for Hubb, Rab for Rabb; a vowel is intercalated in 'Atar for 'Atr, Fateh for Fath, Niamat or Niámat for Ni'mat; a vowel is rejected in Ramzán for Ramazán, Muhamdi for Muhammadi, Shabráti from Shab-i-Barát.

19. Mistaken formations.—Erroneous formations, due to ignorance of Arabic and Persian, are not uncommon. Among those shown in the list are—

Chirághud-dín.	Munído.
Mansullah.	Najíf.
Mumín.	Niyázullah.

Such errors are sometimes found even in high places; a daughter of Aurangzeb, a poetess who wrote under the name of *Makhfi*, was called Zebun-nisá, an impossible combination of Persian and Arabic.

20. Significance of Muhammadan names.—Regarded with reference to their significance, the immense majority of Muhammadan names will be found to have a religious import. Every Muhammadan should properly have an *'alam*, or personal name, chosen from among those of the holy persons of his faith, or from those of the Hebrew and Christian prophets mentioned in the Kurán. To this may be added a *laḳab*, or title, expressive of some religious doctrine, dependence on some holy person, or the like. But there is reason to believe that the distinction between *'alam* and *laḳab* is not generally observed among Indian Musalmáns, and that most of the names in the list are the only ones which their bearers know.

21. **'Alams, or personal names.**—Personal names may be single or double, but none exceed two. Thus, under the letter A, the following are single names taken from the circle of the Prophet and his companions: Ahmad (a name of the Prophet himself), 'Abbás (his uncle), 'Ali (his nephew). Ádam, Ásaf, are names derived from the Hebrew Scriptures. Other such names are Yákúb, Yúsuf, Dáúd, Sulaimán, Is-hák, Ismáíl. 'Ísá (Jesus), Yahya (John the Baptist), and Zakaríya (Zacharias his father) are the only common names of Christian origin in the Kuránic cycle. Names in which two holy persons are joined are more numerous; *e. g.* 'Abbás 'Ali, 'Abbás Husain, Ahmad 'Ali, 'Ali Husain, 'Ali Muhammad. Names having reference to 'Ali, his sons Hasan and Husain, and their descendants the Imáms, are immensely numerous, especially among persons of the Shí'ah sect. Names derived from famous saints are Adham, Bázíd (for Báyazid, and that for Abú-Yazíd), Baháwal (for Baháullah), Bú-'Ali, Muhíyuddín, Buláki, Ajmeri (the famous order of Chishti saints having had their head-quarters at Ajmer), Madár, Malúk, Nakshband, Sálár-bakhsh, Sanái, &c. Names compounded with Imám, Pír, Wali, Makhdúm, and the like, belong to this class, the name of the saint referred to being suppressed. Some religious names are taken from holy places, as Makka, Najaf: others from holy things, as Kurbán, Zul-fikár (the sword of the Prophet, taken at Badr, and afterwards of 'Ali, so called because it had notches on its back like the ridge of the spine).

22. Lakabs, or titles.—The most ordinary form of *laḳab*, or title, is a name compounded of *'Abd* with one of the 99 names of God, or one compounded of *dín* ("faith," "religion") with some appropriate noun or adjective. Where *Ghulám* is used in place of *'Abd*, the following name is always some holy person, and never a name of God; but *'Abd* is sometimes (*e.g.* in 'Abdul-Husain) used with the names of men, though this is probably a solecism.*

The large class of names in which *-bakhsh* forms the second element (always in the passive sense "given by") may be reckoned among *laḳabs* though it rarely happens that a person so called has any separate *'alam*, or personal name.

23. Hindi names borne by Musalmans.—The list includes a considerable number of names of Hindi origin, and therefore not religious, *e g.* Bachu, Bádal, Bádu, Baghi, Bágu, Bairi, Báṉka, Basáwan, Beche, Bhág, Bhaggu, Bhikkha, Bhola, Bhúre, Bihári, Boṛa, Buddhu, Búṭa, Chánd, Chandan, Chaughaṭṭa, Chhedi, Dúbu, Dúnde, &c. These have been already sufficiently described in treating of Hindu names. They are chiefly diminutive or familiar forms.

24. Other secular names.— Besides non-religious names of Indian origin, names drawn from the old heroic legends of Persia are common, *e.g.* Rustam, Suhráb, Bahrám, Isfandiyár, Sikandar.

Martial names, though less frequent than in the lists of Hindu names, are not rare—Sher-dil, Sher-jang, Sher-báz Sháh-báz, Shahín, Pádsháh, Pahlwán, Panáh, Masta, Kesar Khanjar, Shamsher, &c.

A moderate acquaintance with Arabic and Pesian grammar will suffice to explain the construction of almost all the commoner Musalmán names of India; and their meanings are in nearly all instances readily ascertainable from the dictionary.

---

* In the common name 'Abdul-'Alí the word 'Ali is not (as is shown by the prefixed article) the name of the Prophet's nephew, but one of the names of God,—*al-'Alí*, "the Exalted." Possibly 'Abdul-Hasan and 'Abdul-Husain may have originated in a mis, understanding of 'Abdul-'Ali.

NAMES OF HINDUS.

A

Abbhan .	अब्भन ।
Abináshi Rám	अबिनाशी राम ।
Abráj .	अबराज ।
Achala .	अचला ।
Achának	अचानक ।
Achchhar	अच्छर ।
Achhar .	अछर ।
Ádit .	आदित ।
Agan .	अगन ।
Agṛi Rám	अगड़ी राम ।
Ahibaran	अहिबरण ।
Ahimán	अहिमान
Aindha .	ऐंढा ।
Ajab .	अजब ।
Ajáib .	अजाइब (अजायब)।
Ají Rám	अजीत राम ।
Ajít .	अजीत ।
Ajodhya	अजोध्या ।
Ajrál .	अजराल ।
Ajudhya	अजुध्या ।
Akálu .	अकालू ।
Akbar .	अकबर ।
Akhe R m	अखे राम ।
Akshar	अक्षर ।
Ála .	आला ।
Álam .	आलम ।
Albel .	अलबेल ।
Algu .	अलगू ।
Álha .	आल्हा ।
Amán .	अमान ।
Amar .	अमर ।
Amar-chand	अमरचंद ।
Ambar .	अम्बर ।
Ambír .	अंबीर ।
Ami-chand	अमीचंद ।
Ami-Lál	अमीलाल (अमिलाल) ।
Amír .	अमीर ।
Amír-chand	अमीरचंद ।
Amrík .	अमरीक ।
Ánand .	आनन्द ।
Anant Rám	अनन्त राम ।
Angad .	अङ्गद ।
Anganu	अङ्गनू ।
Aneg .	अनेग ।
Anokh .	अनोख ।
Anokhe	अनोखे ।
Antu .	अन्तू ।
Anúp .	अनूप ।
Anúpa .	अनूपा ।
Aparbal	अपरबल ।
Árámi .	आरामी ।
Arbel .	अरबेल ।
Arjun .	अर्जुन ।
Arúṛ .	अरूड़ ।
Ása .	आसा (आशा) ।
Ása-dín	आसादीन ।
Asam .	असम ।
Ása Rám	आसा राम ।
Asharfi-Lál	अशर्फी लाल ।
Asol .	असोल ।
Ássa .	आस्सा ।
At ar .	अतर ।

Atar-chand . अतरचंद ।
Atbal . अतबल (अतिबल)।
A'tma . आत्मा ।
A'tma Rám . आत्मा राम ।
Atr . अत्र ।
Atra . अत्रा ।
Atráj . अतराज ।
Ausán . औसान ।
Auseri . औसेरी ।
Ayodhya . अयोध्या ।

B

Bába-dín . बाबादीन ।
Bábu . . बाबू ।
Bachaí . . बचई ।
Bachan . . बचन ।
Bachchu . बच्चू ।
Bachu-Lál . बचू लाल ।
Bádal . . बादल ।
Badal . . बदल ।
Bádám . . बादाम ।
Badan . . बदन ।
Badhan . . बधन ।
Badháwa . बधावा ।
Badli . . बदली ।
Badlu . . बदलू ।
Badri . . बद्री ।
Badri náth . बदरीनाथ ।
Badrí Náráyan बदरी नारायण ।
Baga . . बगा ।
Bagga . . बग्गा ।
Bágh . . बाघ ।
Bágha . . बाघा ।
Baghel . . बघेल ।
Bahádur . बहादुर ।
Bahál . . बहाल ।
Bahore . . बहोरे ।
Bahori . . बहोरी ।
Bahoru . . बहोरू ।
Bahut Rám . बहुत राम ।
Baijnáth . बैजनाथ ।
Baiju . . बैजू ।
Bainta . . बैंता ।
Bairisál . बैरीसाल(बैरीशाल)
Bhaisáka . बैसाखा ।
Baisákhi . बैसाखी ।
Bajrang . बज्रंग । बजरंग ।
Bakhshi . बखशी (बकसी) ।
Bakhshi Rám बखशी राम ।
Bakhshish . बखशीश (बकसीस)।
Bakht . . बखत ।
Bakhtáwar . बखतावर ।
Bál . . बाल ।
Bálak . . बालक ।
Bálak Rám . बालक राम ।
Balákha . बलाखा ।
Baland . . बलंद ।
Balbhadar . बलभद्र ।
Baldán . . बलदान। बलिदान।
Baldeo . . बलदेव ।
Baldi . . बलदी ।
Bále . . बाले ।
Balgar . . बलगर ।
Bál-Gobind . बालगोबिंद ।
Bali . . बली ।

Báljít .	. बाल जीत।
Bal-karan	. बलकरन(बलिकरण)
Bal-Kishan	. बाल किशन।
Balla .	बल्ला।
Balla Rám	. बल्ला राम।
Ballu .	. बल्लू।
Balmant	. बलमन्त।
Balmi .	. बल्मी।
Bál-mukand (mukund)	बालमुकन्द(मुकुन्द)।
Bálnu .	. बालणू।
Bálu .	. बालू।
Balwant .	. बलवन्त।
Bamanḍa	. बमंडा।
Ban-baṉsi	. बनबंसी।
Bandhan	. बन्धन।
Bandi .	. बन्दी।
Banjára .	. बणजारा।
Báṉka .	. बांका।
Bankaṭ .	. बंकट।
Banna .	. बन्ना।
Baṉsi .	. बंसी।
Barfi .	. बर्फी।
Barjor .	. बरजोर।
Barkat	. बरकत।
Barkha .	. बरखा।
Baryám .	. बरयाम(बरिआम)।
Basákha ..	. बसाखा।
Basáman	. बसामन।
Basant .	. बसन्त।
Basáwa .	. बसावा।
Basáwan	. बसावन।
Básdeo .	. बासदेव।
Bashákha	. बशाखा।

Basti .	. बस्ती।
Basti Rám	. बस्ती राम।
Báẓ .	. बाज़।
Beant .	. बेअन्त।
Becbu .	. बेचू।
Bed Rám	. बेद राम।
Beg .	. बेग।
Bega .	. बेगा।
Bela .	. बेला।
Belam .	. बेलम।
Belár .	. बेलार।
Bella .	बेल्ला।
Beni .	. बेनी।
Beni-bakhsh	. बेनी बखश।
Beni-Mádho	. बेनीमाधो।
Beshákha	. बेशाखा।
Bhabhíkhan	. भभीखन।
Bhabhu .	. भभू।
Bhadaíṉ	. भदईं।
Bhág .	. भाग।
Bhága .	. भागा।
Bhagan .	. भगन।
Bhagat .	. भगत।
Bhaggu	. भग्गू।
Bhág-mal	. भागमल।
Bhagole	. भगोले।
Bhagoti	. भगोती। भगवती।
Bhagu .	. भगू।
Bhagwán	. भगवान।
Bhagwán-dín	. भगवानदीन।
Bhagwán-saháe	भगवान सहाय।
Bhagwant	. भगवन्त।
Bhairo .	. भैरो।
Bhairoṉ	. भैरों।

Bhaj Rám	. भज राम।
Bhama .	. भमा।
Bhamma	. भम्मा (भंमा)।
Bhána .	. भाना।
Bhanga .	. भंगा।
Bhanjan	. भंजन।
Bháram .	. भराम।
Bharat .	. भरत।
Bhárath	. भारथ।
Bháu .	. भाऊ।
Bháu-Lál	. भाऊलाल।
Bhawáni	. भवानी।
Bhawáni-bhíkh	भवानी भीख।
Bhawáni-dín	. भवानी दीन।
Bhawáni-pál	भवानी पाल।
Bhikári .	. भिकारी।
Bhíkha .	. भीखा।
Bhíkha gir	. भीखागिर।
Bhíkham	. भीखन (भीषम)।
Bhikhárí	. भिखारी।
Bhím .	. भीम।
Bhíma .	. भीमा।
Bhimma	. भिम्मा।
Bhodu .	. भोदू।
Bhog Rám	. भोगराम।
Bhoja .	. भोजा।
Bhola .	. भोला।
Bholaí .	. भोलई।
Bholar .	. भोलर।
Bbollu .	. भोल्लू।
Bhondu .	. भोंदू।
Bhoṛa .	. भोड़ा।
Bhosaí .	. भोसई।
Bhuj-bal	. भुजबल।
Bhulan	. भुलन।
Bhulaí- Rám	. भुलई राम।
Bhulla .	. भुल्ला।
Bhúndu	. भून्दू।
Bhúp .	. भूप।
Bhúpa .	. भूपा।
Bhúpál .	. भूपाल।
Bhúra .	. भूरा।
Bhúra Rám	भूरा राम।
Bhúre .	. भूरे।
Bhúri .	. भूरी।
Bhusaí .	. भुसई।
Bichítar	. बिचीतर।
Bichitr .	बिचित्र।
Bihári .	. बिहारी।
Bihári-Lál	. बिहारी लाल।
Bijai .	. बिजै।
Bije .	. बिजे।
Bije Rám	. बिजे राम।
Bikram .	. बिक्रम।
Bikrama	. बिक्रमा।
Bikramajít	. बिक्रमाजीत।
Bikrambar	. बिकरम्बर।
Binda .	. बिन्दा।
Bindában (Bin-daban).	बिन्दाबन।
Bindesari	. बिन्देश्वरी।
Bír .	. बीर।
Bíra .	. बीरा।
Birági .	. बिरागी।
Bír-bal .	. बीरबल।
Bíru .	. बीरू।
Bisákha	. बिसाखा।
Bisál .	. बिसाल।

Bisambhar	. बिसंभर ।
Bisan .	. बिसन ।
Bísan .	. बीसन ।
Bisesar .	. बिसेसर ।
Bisesur .	. बिसेसुर ।
Bishál .	. बिशाल ।
Bishesar	. बिशेसर ।
Bisheshar	. बिशेशर ।
Bishn .	. बिशन ।
Bishna .	. बिशना ।
Bishnáth	. बिशनाथ ।
Bishu .	. बिशु ।
Bishun .	बिशुन ।
Bisrám .	. बिस्राम ।
Bisun .	. बिसुन ।
Bisun-dayál	. बिसुनदयाल ।
Biswanáth	. बिस्वनाथ ।
Biyar .	. बियर ।
Bobad .	. बोबद ।
Bodhi .	. बोधी ।
Bog .	. बोग ।
Bohgi .	. बोह्गी ।
Bora .	. बोड़ा ।
Bore .	. बोड़े ।
Brahm-dayál	. ब्रह्मदयाल ।
Braj-ballabh	. ब्रजबल्लभ ।
Braj-bhúkhan	. ब्रजभूषण ।
Braj-ráj	. ब्रजराज ।
Brij-Lál	. बृजलाल ।
Brikhbhán	. बृषभान ।
Búḍ (Búr)	. बूड ।
Búḍa (Búṛa)	. बूडा ।
Buḍa (Buṛa)	. बुडा ।
Buddhan	. बुद्धन ।
Buddhi	. बुद्धी ।
Buddhu	. बुद्धू ।
Búḍh (Búṛh)	. बूढ ।
Budh .	. बुध ।
Buḍha .	. बुढा ।
Budha .	. बुधा ।
Budhaí	. बुधई ।
Budhan	बुधन ।
Budh-bal	बुधबल (बुधिबल) ।
Budh-Rám	बुधराम (बुधिराम) ।
Budhu .	. बुधू ।
Bújan .	. बूजैन ।
Bujan .	. बुजन ।
Búláki .	. बूलाकी ।
Bunyád	. बुन्याद (बुनियाद) ।
Bunyádi	. बुन्यादी ।
Búṛ (Búḍ)	. बूड़ ।
Búṛa (Búḍa)	. बूड़ा ।
Buṛa (Buḍa)	. बुड़ा ।
Búṛh (Búḍh)	. बूढ़ ।
Buṛha (Buḍha)	बुढ़ा ।
Búṭa .	. बूटा ।
Búṭi .	. बूटी ।
Búṭṭa .	. बूट्टा ।

C

Chain .	. चैन ।
Chain-sukh	. चैनसुख ।
Chaitu .	. चैतू ।
Chakarpán	. चक्रपान ।
Chambel	. चम्बेल ।
Chamman	. चम्मन ।

Chánd .	चांद ।
Chanda .	चंदा ।
Chandan	चन्दन ।
Chandar .	चंदर (चन्द्र) ।
Chandarbhán	चंदरभान ।
Chandar-bir	चंदरबीर ।
Chandar-sekhar	चंद्रशेखर ।
Chandi .	चन्दो ।
Chandi-Lál	चन्दी लाल ।
Chandika	चंदिका ।
Chandka	चंदका ।
Chándnu	चांदनू ।
Channan	चन्नण ।
Charan .	चरण ।
Charanu	चरण ।
Charat .	चड़त ।
Charhat .	चढ़त ।
Charittar	चरित्तर ।
Chatar .	चतर ।
Chataru .	चतरू ।
Chattar .	चत्तर ।
Chatur .	चतुर।
Chaturbhuj	चतुरभुज ।
Chaturi .	चतुरी ।
Chauharja	चौहर्जा ।
Chaukas	चौकस ।
Cháwa .	चावा ।
Cheju .	चेजू ।
Chenchlu	चेंचलू ।
Chenchu	चेंचू ।
Chet .	चेत ।
Cheta .	चेता ।
Chet Rám	चेत राम ।
Chetta .	चेत्ता ।
Chetu .	चेतू ।
Chhabba	छब्बा ।
Chhabíle	छबीले ।
Chhab-náth	छबिनाथ ।
Chhadámi	छदामी ।
Chhailu .	छैलू ।
Chhajja .	छज्जा ।
Chhajju	छज्जू ।
Chháju .	छाजू ।
Chhanga	छंगा ।
Chhangan	छंगन ।
Chhangu	छंगू ।
Chhatarsál	छतरसाल ।
Chhatta	छत्ता ।
Chhattar	छत्तर ।
Chhaṭṭu	छट्टू ।
Chheda .	छेदा ।
Chhedi .	छेदी ।
Chhedu	छेदू ।
Chhián	छिआं ।
Chhíṭan	छीटन ।
Chhítar	छीतर ।
Chhote .	छोटे ।
Chiranji	चिरनजी ।
Chiranju	चिरनजू ।
Chiranju-Lál	चिरनजूलाल ।
Chit-bahál	चितबहाल ।
Chitru .	चित्रू ।
Chittar .	चित्तर ।
Chokha	चोखा ।
Chokhe-Lál	चोखेलाल ।
Chopaí .	चोपई ।
Chugat	चुगत ।
Chúhaṛ	चूहड़ ।

Chuhaṛ . . चुहड़ ।
Chúni-Lál . चनीलाल ।
Chunni . . चुन्नी (चुंनी) ।
Chunni-Lál . चुन्नीलाल ।
Chúr . . चूड़ ।
Chúra . . चूरा ।
Chúraí . . चूरई ।
Chúra-man . चूरामन ।

D

Dadhıbal . दधिबल ।
Ḍágla . . डागला ।
Dal . . दल ।
Ḍál . . डाल ।
Ḍal . . डल ।
Ḍalaí . . डलई ।
Dal-bír . . दलबीर ।
Ḍál-chand . डालचंद ।
Dalel . . दलेल ।
Dale Rám . दले राम ।
Dalíp . . दलीप ।
Dal-jít . . दलजीत ।
Ḍall . . डल्ल ।
Ḍallu Rám . डल्लू राम ।
Dal pat . दलपति ।
Dal-thambhan दलथम्भन ।
Dalt-hamman . दलथम्मन ।
Ḍálu Rám . डालू राम ।
Ḍaluwa . . दलुवा ।
Ḍammar . डम्मर ।
Damodar . दमोदर ।
Dán . . दान ।
Dáni . . दानी ।
Dáni Rám . दानी राम ।
Danna . . दन्ना ।
Dán-sahǽ . दान सहाय ।
Dánu . . दानू ।
Dariáo . . दरिआव(दरियाऊ) ।
Darsan . . दरसन ।
Darshanu . दरशनू ।
Daru . . डरू ।
Dás . . दास ।
Dasanda दसंदा ।
Dasaud . . दसौद ।
Dasauda . दसौदा ।
Dasauṇdha . दसौँधा ।
Dási . . दासी ।
Dáta-dín . दातादीन ।
Dáta Rám . दाता राम ।
Datta . . दत्ता ।
Daula . . दौला ।
Daulat . दौलत (दौलति) ।
Daya . . दया ।
Dayál . . दयाल ।
Daya Rám . दया राम ।
Debi . . देबी ।
Debi-dás . देबी दास ।
Debi dayál . देबी दयाल ।
Debi-dín . देबी दीन ।
Debi-parshád देबी परशाद ।
Debi Rám . देबी राम ।
Debi sahǽ . देबी सहाय ।
Debi-saran . देबी सरन ।
Debiya . देबिया ।
Dei Rám . देई राम ।
Deoki . . देवकी ।

Desa .	. देसा।
Des-ráj .	. देसराज।
Dewa .	देवा।
Dewak Rám	. देवक राम।
Dhan .	. धन।
Dhana .	. धना।
Dhani .	. धनी।
Dhaniya	. धनिया।
Dhanjít .	. धनजीत।
Dhanna .	. धन्ना (धंना)।
Dhanpál	. धनपाल।
Dhanpat	. धनपत (धनपति)
Dhan Rám.	. धन राम।
Dhára .	. धारा।
Dhárajít	. धाराजीत।
Dharam (Dharm)	धरम (धर्म)
Dharam ít	. धरम जीत।
Dhári .	. धारी।
Dharkhan	. धरखन।
Dharma .	. धर्मा।
Dhaukal	. धौकल।
Dhaula .	. धौला।
Dhauṇkal	. धौंकल।
Dhauṇtál	. धौंताल।
Ḍhela .	ढेला।
Ḍhera .	. ढेरा।
Ḍheru .	. ढेरू।
Dhíraj .	. धीरज।
Dhiráu .	धिराऊ।
Ḍhola .	. ढोला।
Dhúmi .	. धूमी।
Dhummu	. धुम्मू।
Dhunda	. धुंदा।
Dhyán .	. ध्यान।
Dhyániyáṇ	. ध्यानियां।
Dídár .	. दीदार।
Ḍíḍo	. डीडो।
Ḍígh Rám	. डीघ राम।
Dillu .	. दिल्लू।
Dílmoṛ .	. दीलमोड़।
Dilpat .	. दिलपत।
Dil-sukh	दिलसुख।
Dilwant	. दिलवन्त।
Dína .	. दीना।
Ḍínga .	. डींगा।
Díp .	. दीप।
Dípan .	. दीपन।
Dípu .	. दीपू।
Dirg pál	. दिर्गपाल।
Díwán .	. दीवान।
Díwána .	. दीवाना।
Diwánu	. दिवानू।
Diya .	. दिया।
Ḍohan .	. डोहन।
Ḍongar	. डोंगर।
Drag-pál	. द्रगपाल।
Dripnáth	. द्रिपनाथ।
Dubáru	. दुबारू।
Ḍugar .	. डुगर।
Dukh-chhor	. दुखछोर।
Dúla .	. दूला।
Dula .	. दुला।
Dulár .	. दुलार।
Duli-chand	. दुलीचंद।
Dúli-chand	. दूलीचंद।
Dúlla .	. दूल्ला।
Dulla .	. दुल्ला।
Dullam .	. दुल्लम।

Dúllo .	दूल्लो ।
Dund .	दुंद ।
Duni-chand	दुनीचंद ।
Duniyáṇ .	दुनियां ।
Dunni .	दुन्नी ।
Durbali .	दुर्बली ।
Durg .	दुर्ग ।
Durga .	दुर्गा ।
Durga Rám	दुर्गा राम ।
Dúrjan .	दूर्जन ।
Durjan .	दुर्जन ।
Durmech	दुर्मेच ।
Dusandha	दुसंधा ।
Dwárika	द्वारिका ।
Dwárika-dás	द्वारिका दास ।

F

Fakíra .	फकीरा ।
Fakír chand	फकीर चंद ।
Farangi .	फरंगी ।
Fate-bahádur	फते बहादुर ।
Fatúri .	फतूरी ।
Fatta .	फत्ता ।
Faṭte .	फत्ते ।
Fattu .	फत्तू ।
Fauju .	फौजू ।
Faujdár	फौजदार ।
Fazal-dín	फजल दीन ।
Farmán .	फर्मान ।
Fursat .	फुर्सत ।
Fursati .	फुर्सती ।

G

Gahal .	गहल ।
Gain .	गैन ।
Gainḍa .	गैंडा ।
Gaja .	गजा ।
Gajadhar	गजाधर ।
Gajan .	गजन ।
Gaje .	गजे ।
Gajjan .	गज्जन ।
Gaj-ráj .	गजराज ।
Gajráte .	गजराते ।
Gambhír	गम्भीर ।
Gana .	गणा ।
Ganḍa .	गंडा ।
Gáṇdha .	गांधा ।
Ganes .	गनेस ।
Ganesh	गणेश ।
Ganesha	गणेशा ।
Ganeshi	गणेशी ।
Ganga .	गङ्गा ।
Ganga Bisun	गंगा बिसुन ।
Ganga dhar	गंगाधर ।
Ganga-dín	गंगादीन ।
Ganga-parshád	गंगा परशाद ।
Ganga Rám	गंगा राम ।
Ganga-saháe	गंगा सहाय ।
Gangu .	गंगू ।
Gangua	गंगुआ ।
Ganiyáṇ	गणियां ।

Ganpat .	गणपत (गणपति)।
Garbha .	गरभा।
Garíb Rám	गरीब राम।
Gaṭṭu .	गट्टू।
Gaú datt	गऊदत्त।
Gauhar-chand	गौहर चंद।
Gaun .	गौन।
Gauri .	गौरी।
Gauri Shankar	गौरी शंकर।
Gaya-dín	गयादीन।
Ghamanḍa	घमंडा।
Ghanaiya	घनैया।
Ghan-shyám	घनश्याम।
Ghánṯha .	घांथा।
Ghaṛ-syám	घड़स्याम।
Ghási .	घासी।
Ghási Rám	घासी राम।
Ghasíṭa .	घसीटा।
Gheráu .	घेराऊ।
Ghethal .	घेथल।
Ghisaí .	घिसई।
Ghísan .	घीसन।
Ghisiáwan	घिसिआवन।
Ghísu .	घीसू।
Ghoṭa .	घोटा।
Ghụla .	घुला।
Ghumí .	घुमी।
Ghúru .	घूरू।
Gíhalli .	गोहल्ली।
Girdhar .	गिरधर।
Girdhári .	गिरधारी।
Girwar .	गिरवर।
Gobardhan	गोबर्धन।
Gobind .	गोबिंद।
Gobinda	गोबिंदा।
Gobind-parshád	गोबिंद परशाद।
Gog-náth	गोगनाथ।
Gokul .	गोकुल।
Gokula .	गोकुला।
Gond .	गोंद।
Gopál .	गोपाल।
Gopál Rám	गोपाल राम।
Gopi .	गोपी।
Gopi-náth	गोपीनाथ।
Gopi Rám	गोपी राम।
Gopiya .	गोपिया।
Goptár*	गोपतार।
Granthi	ग्रंथी।
Gudaṛ .	गुदड़।
Gúgan .	गूगन।
Gúgan Ram	गूगन राम
Gújar .	गूजर।
Gujar .	गुजर।
Gujjar .	गुज्जर।
Guláb .	गुलाब।
Gulába .	गुलाबा।
Gulzár .	गुलज़ार।
Gulzári	गुलज़ारी।
Gumán .	गुमान।
Gumáni .	गुमानी।
Gun raj	गुनराज।
Gupál .	गुपाल।
Gupála .	गुपाला।
Gur-bakhsh	गुर बखश।
Gur-bhaj	गुरभज।
Gur-datt	गुरदत्त।

* Probably for Guftár گفتار

Gur-dayál	गुरदयाल ।
Gur-din	गुरदीन ।
Gur-ditt	गुरदित्त ।
Gur-mukh	गुरमुख ।
Gur-sukh	गुरसुख ।
Gusáún	गुसाऊँ ।
Guṭa	गुटा ।
Guṭṭa	गुट्टा ।
Gyán	ग्यान (ज्ञान) ।
Gyána	ग्याना ।

H

Habchal	हबचल ।
Hájra	हाजरा ।
Hákam	हाकम ।
Hákim	हाकिम ।
Hákim Ráe	हाकिम राय ।
Háku	हाकू ।
Hamír	हमीर ।
Hannu	हन्नू ।
Hansa	हंसा ।
Hans-ráj	हंसराज ।
Hans Rám	हंस राम ।
Hanumán	हनुमान ।
Hanumán-datt	हनुमान दत्त ।
Hanumant	हनुमन्त ।
Hanwant	हनवन्त ।
Har	हर ।
Harasya	हरस्या ।
Har-bakhsh	हरबख्श ।
Har-bans	हरबंस ।
Har-bhagat	हरभगत ।
Har-bhaj	हरभज ।
Har bhajan	हरभजन ।
Har-bhanjan	हरभजन ।
Har-chain	हरचैन ।
Har-chand	हरचंद ।
Har-charan	हरिचरन ।
Har-dáhin	हरि दाहिन ।
Har-dás	हरदास ।
Har-datt	हरदत्त ।
Har-dayál	हरदयाल ।
Har-deo	हरदेव ।
Harde Rám	हरदे राम ।
Har-dhyán	हरध्यान ।
Har-dín	हरदीन ।
Har-ditt	हरदित्त ।
Har dwár	हरिद्वार ।
Hardwári	हरद्वारी ।
Har-Gobin	हरगोबिन ।
Har-Gobind	हरगोबिंद ।
Har-gyán	हरग्यान ।
Hari	हरी ।
Hari-Har	हरिहर ।
Harí Rám	हरि राम ।
Hariya	हरिया ।
Har-jas	हरजस ।
Har-ji	हरजी ।
Har Kisun	हरि किसुन ।
Har-Lál	हरिलाल ।
Har-nám	हरनाम ।
Har-Nand	हरनन्द ।
Har-nath	हरनाथ ।
Har-pál	हरिपाल ।
Har-parshád	हरपरशाद ।
Har-phúl	हरफूल ।

Har-saháe . हरसहाय ।
Har-saran . हरसरन ।
Har-sukh . हरसुख ।
Hastu . . हस्तू ।
Hazára . . हज़ारा ।
Hazári . . हज़ारी ।
Hazúra . . हज़ूरा ।
Hem . . हेम ।
Hem raj . हेमराज ।
Het Rám . हेत राम ।
Hímanchal . हीमंचल ।
Himmat . . हिम्मत ।
Hindu . . हिंदु ।
Híra . . हीरा ।
Híra-Lál . हीरा लाल ।
Hira-man . हीरा मनि ।
Híra-Nand . हीरा नन्द ।

Hirde Rám . हिर्दे राम ।
Híri . . हीरी ।
Hirwa . . हिरवा ।
Holu . . होलू ।
Hori . . होरी ।
Horol . . होरोल ।
Hubdár . . हुबदार ।
Hub-Lál हुबलाल ।
Hukam . . हुकम ।
Hukam-chand. हुकम चंद ।
Hukma . हुक्मा ।
Hukúmat-ráe . हुकूमतराय ।
Hulaí . . हुलई ।
Hulás . . हुलास ।
Hulási . . हुलासी ।
Hunta . . हुन्ता ।
Hushyár . हुशयार ।

I

Ichchha Rám . इच्छा राम ।
Imrat . . इम्रत ।
Inchha . . इन्छा ।
Indar . . इंदर ।
Indar-bír . इंदरबीर ।
Indar-jít . . इंदरजीत ।
Indar-man . इंद्रमनि ।
Indar-pál . इंदर पाल ।

Indráj . . इंदराज ।
Ísar . . ईसर ।
Íshar . . ईशर ।
Íshri . . ईशरी ।
Íshwar . . ईश्वर ।
Íshwari . . ईश्वरी ।
Ísru . . ईस्रू ।
Isuri . . ईसुरी ।

J

Jabbar . . जब्बर ।
Jabṛa . . जबड़ा ।
Jaeshri . . जएशरी ।
Jag . . जग ।

Jagadamba . जगदम्बा ।
Jagan . . जगन ।
Jagan-náth . जगन्नाथ ।
Jagarnáth . जगरनाथ ।

Jagat .	. जगत ।
Jag-bandan	. जगबंदन ।
Jag-datt	. जगदत्त ।
Jag-deo .	. जगदेव ।
Jagesar .	. जगेसर ।
Jag-mohan	. जगमोहन ।
Jag pál .	. जगपाल ।
Jag-Rám	. जगराम ।
Jagwant	. जगवन्त ।
Jahán .	. जहान ।
Jahángír	. जहँागीर ।
Jahwár*	. जहवार ।
Jai (Jay)	. जै (जय) ।
Jai datt .	. जै दत्त ।
Jai-Gobind	. जैगोबिंद ।
Jai-Gupál	. जै गुपाल ।
Jai-jai Rám	. जै जै राम ।
Jai-karan	. जयकर्ण ।
Jai-Kisun	. जै किसुन ।
Jai-Lál .	. जै लाल ।
Jai-mal .	. जै मल ।
Jai-mangal	. जै मङ्गल ।
Jai-nandan	. जै नन्दन ।
Jai-náth .	. जै नाथ ।
Jai-pál .	. जै पाल ।
Jai-sukh	. जै सुख ।
Jal .	. जल ।
Jálpu .	. जाल्पू ।
Jálu .	. जालू ।
Jám .	. जाम ।
Jamaiyat	. जमैयत ।
Jamal .	. जमल ।
Jaman .	. जमन ।
Jamand .	. जमंद ।
Jamíit .	. जमीइत ।
Jamít .	. जमीत ।
Jamna-parshád	जमना परशाद ।
Jamuna	. जमुना ।
Janbed .	. जनबेद ।
Janga .	. जंगा ।
Jangali .	. जंगली ।
Jangi .	. जंगी ।
Jangi-Lál	. जंगी लाल ।
Jánki .	. जानकी ।
Jánki-dás	. जानकी दास ।
Jánki-parshád	जानकी परशाद ।
Jas-bír .	. जसबीर ।
Jas karan	. जसकरन ।
Jasmant	. जसमंत ।
Jas-Rám	. जसराम ।
Jaswant	. जसवन्त ।
Játa .	. जाता ।
Jaṭdhári	. जटधारी।जटाधारी।
Jatiwant	. जतिवन्त ।
Jaudh .	. जौध ।
Jauhari .	. जौहरी ।
Jaurákhan	. जौराखन ।
Jawáhara	. जवाहरा ।
Jawáhir .	. जवाहिर ।
Jawand	. जवंद ।
Jayanta .	. जयंता ।
Jhábar .	. झाबर ।
Jhabba .	. झब्बा ।
Jhíbu .	. झाबू ।
Jhagaṛ .	. झगड़ ।
Jhágíra .	. झागीरा ।

* For Jawáhir.

Jhakhri	. झखरी ।
Jhám .	. झाम ।
Jhámṭu .	. झामटू ।
Jhanḍ .	. झंड ।
Jhanḍa .	. झंडा ।
Jhanḍu .	. झंडू ।
Jhangan	. झंगन ।
Jharihag	. झरिहग ।
Jharihak-Rám	. झरिहक राम ।
Jhaṭiya .	. झटिया ।
Jháu .	. झाऊ ।
Jhújhan .	. झूझन ।
Jhúthar .	. झूथर ।
Jiáwan .	. जिआवन ।
Jíman .	. जीमन ।
Jimi-pál .	. जिमिपाल ।
Jinda .	. जिंदा ।
Jí-Rám .	. जीराम ।
Jí-sukh .	. जीसुख ।
Jít .	. जीत ।
Jíta .	. जीता ।
Jít-Rám .	. जीत राम ।
Jitwár .	. जितवार ।
Jíun .	. जीउण ।
Jíut .	. जीउत ।
Jíwa .	. जीवा ।
Jíwan .	. जीवन ।
Jíwand .	. जीवंद ।
Jíwa-Rám	. जीवा राम ।
Jiwrákhan	. जिवराखन ।
Jiya-Lál	. जियालाल ।
Jíya-Rám	. जीया राम ।
Jodh .	. जोध ।
Jodha .	. जोधा ।
Johgal .	. जोहगल ।
Jokha .	. जोखा ।
Jokhan .	. जोखन ।
Jokhe .	. जोखे ।
Jokhu .	. जोखू ।
Joṇra .	जौंड़ा ।
Jora .	. जोरा ।
Jorâwar	. जोरावर ।
Jori .	. जोरी ।
Joti .	. जोती ।
Jot Rám	जोत राम ।
Jugal .	. जुगल ।
Jugal-kishor	. जुगल किशोर ।
Jug-ráj .	. जुगराज ।
Juhár* .	. जुहार ।
Julphi .	. जुल्फी ।
Jurákhan	. जुराखन ।
Jurâwal .	. जुरावल ।
Juṛáwan	. जुड़ावन ।
Júṭhan .	. जूठन ।
Juwána	. जुवाना ।
Juwand .	. जुवंद ।
Jwála .	. ज्वाला ।
Jwála-parshád	. ज्वाला परशाद ।
Jwár* .	. जवार ।

K

Kábul .	. काबुल ।
Kadam .	. कदम ।

* Jawáhir

Kadher . . कढेर ।
Káhan . . काहन ।
Kailás . . कैलास ।
Káka . . काका ।
Káku . . काकू ।
Kála . . काला ।
Kalap-náth . कलपनाथ ।
Kali . . काली ।
Káli-charan . काली चरन ।
Káli-dín . काली दीन ।
Kálika . . कालिका ।
Kálka . . कालका ।
Kallu . . कल्लू ।
Kálu . . कालू ।
Kalyán . . कल्यान ।
Kalyáne . कल्याने ।
Kamal . . कमल ।
Kamla-pati . कमलापती ।
Kamle . . कमले ।
Kámta . . कामता ।
Kámta-parshád कामता परशाद ।
Kán . . कान (कांन) ।
Kanchan . कंचन ।
Kandhaí . कंधई ।
Kandhái . कंधाई ।
Kandhaiya . कंधैया ।
Kandhaiya-bakhsh . कंधैया बखश ।
Kandhára . कंधारा ।
Kangan . कंगन ।
Kánh . . कान्ह ।
Kánha . . कान्हा ।
Kanhai Lál . कन्हई लाल ।
Kanhaiya . कन्हैया ।
Kanhaiya Lál कन्हैया लाल ।
Kannu . . कन्नू ।
Kánsí Rám . कांसी राम ।
Kapúr . . कपूर ।
Karam-chand . करम चंद ।
Karm . . कर्म ।
Karn . . कर्ण ।
Karore . . करोड़े ।
Karori . . करोरी ।
Kashmíri . कश्मीरी ।
Kási (Káshí) . कासी (काशी) ।
Kásí Ram . कासीराम ।
Katha . . कथा ।
Katwáru . कतवारू ।
Kaulu . . कौलू ।
Kaura . . कौड़ा ।
Kauru . . कौड़ू ।
Kawal . . कवल ।
Kedár-náth . केदारनाथ ।
Kedáru . . केदारू ।
Kehar . . केहर ।
Kehri . . केहरी ।
Kenu . . केनू ।
Kesab . . केसब ।
Kesar . . केसर ।
Keshar . . केशर ।
Kesho . . केशो ।
Kesho Rám . केशो राम ।
Kesra . . केसरा ।
Kesri . . केसरी ।
Kesru . . केसरू ।
Kewal . . केवल ।
Khabar . . खबर ।
Khagole . खगोले ।

Khaira .	. खैरा ।
Khairáti .	. खैराती ।
Khalak .	. खलक ।
Khanaín	. खनऊं ।
Khandhára	. खंधारा ।
Khanjan	. खंजन ।
Khaṛag .	. खड़ग ।
Khaṛag-jít	. खड़गजीत ।
Khaṛak-bír	. खड़कबीर ।
Khaṛga .	. खड़गा ।
Khaṛku .	. खड़कू ।
Khazán .	. खज़ान ।
Khedu .	. खेदू ।
Khem .	. खेम ।
Khem-anand	. खेमानन्द ।
Khem Rám	. खेम राम ।
Kheta .	. खेता ।
Khewan	. खेवन ।
Khíman .	. खीमन ।
Khíwan .	. खीवन ।
Khoju .	. खोजू ।
Khúbi .	. खूबी ।
Khumán	. खुमान ।
Khumání	खुमानी ।
Khusál .	. खुसाल ।
Khushál	. खुशाल ।
Khushhál	. खुशहाल ।
Khushháli Rám	खुशहाली राम ।
Khushi Rám	. खुशी राम ।
Khushiya	. खुशिया ।
Khusiál .	. खुसिआल ।
Khusyál	. खुस्याल ।
Khyáli .	. ख्याली ।
Khyáli Rám	. ख्याली राम ।
Kiḍḍa .	. किड्डा ।
Kindar .	. किन्दर ।
Kiránt .	. किरान्त ।
Kíṛí .	. कीड़ी ।
Kirpa .	किर्पा ।
Kisan .	. किसन ।
Kisan sahác	. किसन सहाय ।
Kishan-bal	. किशन बल ।
Kishor .	. किशोर ।
Kishora	. किशोरा ।
Kishun	. किशुन ।
Kisun .	. किसुन ।
Kiṭṭhu .	. किट्ठू ।
Komil .	. कोमिल ।
Kor .	. कोर ।
Kripa-Rám	कृपा राम ।
Kripál .	. कृपाल ।
Krishna	. कृषणा ।
Kumal .	. कुमल ।
Kumarpál	. कुमरपाल ।
Kundan	. कुन्दन ।
Kunjan	. कुंजन ।
Kunjar .	. कुजर ।
Kuṉwar	कुंवर ।
Kuṉwar Sain	कुंवर सैन ।
Kuṛa .	. कुड़ा ।
Kuṛe .	. कुड़े ।
Kúṛhe .	. कूढ़े ।
Kusahar-dín	. कुसहर दीन ।
Kusal .	कुसल ।
Kushál .	. कुशाल ।
Kushála	. कुशाला ।
Kusyál .	. कुस्याल ।
Kusyáli	. कुस्याली ।

L

Lábh .	. लाभ ।
Lachhi Rám	. लच्छी राम ।
Lachhiman	. लच्छिमन ।
Lachhman	. लछमन ।
Lachhu .	. लछू ।
Laddha .	. लद्धा ।
Ladúri .	. लदूरी ।
Lahan .	. लहण ।
Lahanu .	. लहनू ।
Láhauri .	. लाहौरी ।
Lahina .	. लहिना ।
Lahna .	. लहना (लहणा) ।
Lahri .	. लहरी ।
Laihna .	. लैहना ।
Láik .	. लायक ।
Lajja-Rám	. लज्जा राम ।
Lakha .	. लषा ।
Lakhmi-dás	. लखमी दास ।
Lahhmín-chand	लखमींचंद ।
Lakh-náth	लखनाथ ।
Lakshiman	. लच्छिमन ।
Lakshman	. लच्छमन ।
Lakshmi-dás	. लच्छमी दास ।
Lakshmi-Náráyan	. लच्छमी नारायण ।
Lál .	. लाल ।
Lála . .	. लाला ।
Lála Rám	. लाला राम ।
Lalak .	. ललक ।
Lál-chand	. लालचंद ।
Lálji .	. लालजी ।
Láljit .	. लालजीत ।
Lálju .	. लालजू ।
Lalli .	. लल्ली ।
Lallu .	. लल्लू ।
Lálta .	. लालता ।
Lálta-parshád	लालता परशाद ।
Lálu .	. लाल ।
Lalwa .	. ललवा ।
Lana .	. लान ।
Lankush	. लंकुश ।
Lashman .	. लशमन ।
Lashman-dás	. लशमन दास ।
Lauṭan .	. लौटन ।
Lehna .	. लेहना (लेहणा) ।
Lekha .	. लेखा ।
Lekh Rám	. लेख राम ।
Likal .	. लिकल ।
Likhḍu .	. लिखड ।
Likhma .	. लिखमा ।
Líla-dhar	. लीलाधर ।
Lobhi .	. लोभी ।
Lodi .	. लोदी ।
Lokaí .	. लोकई ।
Loṛída .	. लोड़ीदा ।
Ludar .	. लुदर ।
Lúri .	. लरी ।

M

Madan .	. मदन ।
Madári .	. मदारी ।
Madháb	. मधाब ।
Madhábba	. मधाब्बा ।

Mádho . . माधो ।
Mádho Rám . माधो राम ।
Mádu . . माडू ।
Magan-Lál . मगन लाल ।
Magar . . मगर ।
Maghar . . मघर ।
Máh . . माह ।
Maha . . महा ।
Maha-bal . महाबल ।
Maha-bír . महाबीर ।
Mahadeo . महादेव ।
Maha-jít . महाजीत ।
Mahalli , . महल्ली ।
Maháṉ . . महां ।
Mahanand . महानन्द ।
Mahar . . महर ।
Maha Rám . महा राम ।
Maha-sukh . महासुख ।
Mahbúb . महबूब ।
Mahendar . महेंदर ।
Mahes . . महेस ।
Mahesar . महेसर ।
Mahesh-bakhsh महेश बखश ।
Mahessa . महेससा ।
Mahíp . . महीप ।
Mahi-pál . महीपाल ।
Mahípat . महीपत ।
Máhma . . माहमा ।
Mahráj . . महराज ।
Mahtáb . . महताब ।
Maiku . . मैकू ।
Maiya . . मैया (मईया) ।
Máiya . . माइया ।
Majja . . मज्जा ।
Majla . . मजला ।
Majla Rám . मजला राम ।
Majlis . . मजलिस ।
Mákhan . माखन ।
Makkhan मक्खन ।
Makkhan Lál . मक्खन लाल ।
Makrand . मक्रंद ।
Maksúdan . मकसूदन ।
Makund . मकुंद ।
Mal . . मल ।
Mála . . माला ।
Malha . . मलहा ।
Máli . . माली ।
Mall . . मल्ल ।
Malla . . मल्ला ।
Málu . . मालू ।
Malúk . . मलूक ।
Malúka . मलूका ।
Malúk Rám . मलूक राम ।
Mám-chand . मामचंद ।
Mám-ráj मामराज ।
Mán . . मान ।
Mána . . माना ।
Man bhar . मनभर ।
Man-bháwan मनभावन ।
Man-bír . मनबीर ।
Man-bodh . मनबोध ।
Máṉde . . मांदे ।
Man-díp . मनदीप ।
Mangal . मङ्गल ।
Mangali . मङ्गली ।
Mangal-parshád मङ्गल परशाद ।
Mangalu . मङ्गलू ।
Mangru . मंग्रू ।

Máṉh .	मांह ।
Mánik .	मानिक ।
Mani Rám	मनि राम ।
Man-jít .	मनजीत ।
Máṉkhan	मांखन ।
Man-mohan	मनमोहन ।
Manohar	मनोहर ।
Man-phúl	मनफूल ।
Man-ráj	मनराज ।
Man Rám	मन राम ।
Mansa	मनसा ।
Mansa Rám	मनसा राम ।
Man-sukh	मनसुख ।
Mansúri	मन्सूरी ।
Mánu .	मानु ।
Manusa .	मनुसा ।
Máṛe .	माड़े ।
Mraík .	मरीक ।
Masa .	मसा ।
Massa .	मस्सा ।
Mastáb .	मस्ताब ।
Mastán .	मस्तान ।
Mastbír .	मस्तबीर ।
Mastu .	मस्तू ।
Matáb .	मताब ।
Máta-bakhsh	माता बखश ।
Máta-bhíkh	माता भीख ।
Máta dín	माता दीन ।
Mataú .	मतऊ ।
Mathura	मथुरा ।
Mathura-dín	मथुरा दीन ।
Mathura-par-shád	मथुरापरशाद ।
Mathuri	मथुरी ।
Matole .	मतोले ।
Mattáb .	मत्ताब ।
Mawási	मवासी ।
Maya .	मया ।
Maya Rám	मया राम ।
Mayya	मय्या ।
Med .	मेद ।
Meda .	मेदा ।
Medu .	मेदू ।
Megh .	मेघ ।
Mehar .	मेहर ।
Mehar-chand	मेहरचंद ।
Mehdi-din	मेहदी दीन ।
Mehrwán	मेहरवान ।
Meṛaí (Meraí)	मेड़ई (मेरई) ।
Mewa .	मेवा ।
Mewa-Lál	मेवा लाल ।
Miha .	मिहा ।
Míha .	मीहा ।
Míháṉ .	मीहां ।
Mihíṉ Lal	मिहीं लाल ।
Mihrbán	मिहरबान ।
Mihr-chand	मिहरचंद ।
Milkhi .	मिलखी ।
Minṭhu	मिंठू ।
Misiri .	मिसिरी ।
Misra .	मिस्रा ।
Misrí .	मिश्री ।
Mit .	मित ।
Mít .	मीत ।
Mita .	मिता ।
Mítai .	मितई ।
Miṭhu Lál	मिठू लाल ।
Mitt .	मित्त ।

Míṭṭhu .	. मिट्ठू ।
Miya .	. मिया ।
Mohan .	. मोहन ।
Mohar .	. मोहर ।
Mohkam	. मोहकम ।
Mohobat	. मोहोबत ।
Moji Rám	. मोजी राम ।
Molak .	. मोलक ।
Molar .	. मोलर ।
Molhu .	. मोल्हू ।
Moman .	. मोमन ।
Mota .	. मोता ।
Moti .	. मोती ।
Moti Rám	. मोती राम ।
Mugali .	. मुगली ।
Mukand	. मुकंद ।
Mukh Rám	. मुख राम ।
Mukta .	. मुक्ता ।
Mukta-parshád	मुक्ता परशाद ।
Muktáyal	. मुक्तायल ।
Mukti Rám	मुक्ति राम ।
Mukund	. मकुंद ।
Mukuṭ .	. मुकुट ।
Mul .	. मुल ।
Mula .	. मुला ।
Múla .	. मूला ।
Muláim	. मुलायम ।
Múl-chand	. मूलचंद ।
Multán .	. मुल्तान ।
Multáni	. मुल्तानी ।
Múlu .	. मूल ।
Muna .	. मुना ।
Mundra	. मुंद्रा ।
Munna .	. मुन्ना ।
Murári Lal	. मुरारि लाल ।
Murli .	. मुर्ली ।
Murli-dhar	. मुर्लीधर ।
Múrti .	. मूरती ।
Musaddi	. मुसद्दी ।
Mutasaddi	. मुतसद्दी ।
Muṭru .	. मुड्रू (मुटरू) ।

N

Nabáb .	. नबाब ।
Nabd Rám	. नब्द राम ।
Nádán .	. नादान ।
Nádṛu .	. नादड़ू ।
Nágar .	. नागर ।
Nagesar	. नगेसर ।
Nagína .	. नगीना ।
Nágo .	. नागो ।
Nag-pál	. नगपाल ।
Náhar .	. नाहर ।
Nain .	. नैन ।
Nain sukh	. नैनसुख ।
Naipál .	. नैपाल ।
Nakhru	. नखरू ।
Nának .	. नानक ।
Nánaku	. नानकू ।
Nand .	. नन्द ।
Nandan	. नन्दन ।
Nand-kishor	. नन्द किशोर ।
Nand-kumár	. नन्द कुमार ।
Nand-lál	. नन्द लाल ।
Nand Rám	. नन्द राम ।

Nandu .	. नन्दू।
Nanhe .	. नन्हे।
Nánik .	. नानिक।
Nánik Rám	. नानिक राम।
Nanku .	. ननकू।
Nannu .	. नन्नू।
Nánu .	. नानू।
Naránne .	. नरांने।
Náráyan .	. नारायण।
Naráyan .	. नरायण।
Naráyan-Dás	. नरायण दास।
Naráyan-dín	नरायण दीन।
Naráyanu	. नरायणू।
Narbhán	. नरभान।
Nar-bír .	. नरबीर।
Nar-singh	. नरसिंह।
Náth .	. नाथ।
Natha .	. नथा।
Nathaí .	. नथई।
Náthu Ram	. नाथू राम।
Nattha .	. नत्था।
Natthan .	नत्थन।
Natthu .	. नत्थू।
Nátthu .	. नाट्ठू।
Natthuwa	. नत्थवा।
Naubat .	. नौबत।
Naurang	. नौरंग।
Nauranga	. नौरंगा।
Nawáb .	. नवाब।
Nawal .	. नवल।
Nayan .	. नयन।
Nayana .	. नयणा।
Neki-Rám	. नेकी राम।
Nek Rám	नेक राम।
Nekse .	नेकसे।
Neta .	. नेता।
Netr .	. नेत्र।
Net-Rám	. नेत राम।
Netu .	. नेतू।
Niddhi .	. निद्धी।
Nidha .	. निधा।
Nidhán .	. निधान।
Nihál .	. निहाल।
Nihá'a .	. निहाला।
Nihál-chand	. निहालचंद।
Nihálu .	. निहालु।
Nika .	. निका।
Nímbar	. नीम्बर।
Nirahu .	. निरहु।
Niranjan	. निरंजन।
Nirbho .	. निर्भो।
Nirghan	. निर्घन।
Nirmal .	. निर्मल।
Nirmán	. निर्मान।
Nirpat .	. निरपत (निरपति)।
Nohar .	. नोहर।
Nohari .	. नोहरी।
Nok .	. नोक।
Noraí .	. नोरई।
Nurang .	. नुरंग।
Nurdhan	. नुरधन।

O

Ori .	. ओरी।

P

Padam .	. पदम ।
Padárath	. पदारथ ।
Padmán̲	. पदमां ।
Paháṛ .	. पहाड़ ।
Pahinju .	. पहिंजू ।
Pahlád .	. पहलाद ।
Fabli .	. पहली ।
Pahlwán	. पहलवान ।
Pahunchi Rám	पहुंचो राम ।
Pákhar .	. पाखर ।
Pál .	. पाल ।
Pála .	. पाला ।
Paljham	. पलझम ।
Palṭún̲ .	. पलटूं ।
Pancham	. पंचम ।
Panjáb .	. पंजाब ।
Panju .	. पजू ।
Parameshwar	. परमेश्वर ।
Param-sukh	. परमसुख ।
Paras Rám	. परस राम ।
Parautı .	. परौती ।
Parbat .	. परबत ।
Parbati .	. परबती ।
Pargane .	. परगने ।
Parítam	. परीतम ।
Parma .	. परमा ।
Parmanand	. परमानन्द ।
Parmesuri-din	. पर्मेसुरीदीन ।
Parmod .	. पर्मोद ।
Parsádí .	. पर्सादी ।
Parsan .	. पर्सण ।
Parshád .	. पर्शाद ।
Pars Rám	. पर्स राम ।

Parsu .	. पर्सू ।
Partáb .	. पर्ताब ।
Partáp .	. पर्ताप ।
Parwan	. परवन ।
Parwati	. परवती ।
Páṭan-dín	. पाटन दीन ।
Paṭhánu	. पठानू ।
Pat Rám	. पत राम ।
Pem .	. पेम ।
Pem-ráj	. पेम राज ।
Phaga .	. फगा ।
Phagu .	. फगू ।
Phaggu .	. फग्गू ।
Phahalli	. फहल्ली ।
Phaili .	. फैली ।
Phailo .	. फैलो ।
Phállu .	. फाल्लू ।
Phamman	. फम्मन ।
Phándi .	. फांदी ।
Phangan	. फंगन ।
Phangu	. फंगू ।
Phenkún̲	. फेंकू ।
Phíhanna	. फीहन्ना ।
Phíku .	. फीकू ।
Phúl .	. फूल ।
Phúla .	. फूला ।
Phúl-chand	. फूलचंद ।
Phulli .	. फ़ुल्ली ।
Phuman	. फुमन ।
Phúman	. फूमन ।
Phundan	. फुंदन ।
Pinjha .	. पिंझा ।
Pirág .	. पिराग ।

Pirán-sukh	. पिरान सुख।
Pirthi-pál	. पिर्थी पाल।
Píru .	. पीरू।
Pitaí .	. पितई।
Pítam .	. पीतम।
Pitambar	. पितंबर।
Pítámbar	. पीतांबर।
Pitthu .	. पित्थू।
Pohp .	. पोह्प।
Pohpi .	. पोह्पी।
Pohu .	. पोह्ु।
Pokhan .	. पोखन।
Prabh-dayál	. प्रभ दयाल।
Prabhu .	. प्रभू (प्रभु।)
Prabhu-dín	. प्रभू दीन।
Praddu .	. प्रद्दु।
Pradhána	. प्रधाना।
Prág .	. प्राग।
Prág-dín	. प्राग दीन।
Prahlád	. प्रह्लाद।
Prakás Ráe	. प्रकास राय।
Pramod .	. प्रमोद।
Prán .	. प्रान।
Prán-pat	. प्रानपत।
Prán-sukh	. प्रान सुख।
Prasiddh Nárá-yan .	. प्रसिद्ध नारायण।
Pratáp .	. प्रताप।
Prayág .	. प्रयाग।
Prem .	. प्रेम।
Prem-sukh	. प्रेम सुख।
Príthi .	. पृथी।
Prithi-pál	. पृथी पाल।
Prithi-raj	. पृथी राज।
Prít Rám	. प्रीत राम।
Pudaí .	. पुदई।
Púdhaí .	. पूधई।
Puhp .	. पुह्प।
Punbhadar	. पुनभदर।
Punnu .	. पुन्नू।
Puraí .	. पुरई।
Púran .	. पूरन (पूरण)।
Purusottam	. पुरुसोत्तम।
Púsu .	. पूसू।
Pyára .	. प्यारा।
Pyáre .	. प्यारे।
Pyáre-Lál	. प्यारे लाल।

R

Rabbal .	. रब्बल।
Rabela .	. रबेला।
Rabi-Lál	. रबिलाल।
Rachpál	. रचपाल।
Raddhu	. रद्धू।
Rádha .	. राधा।
Rádha Kishan	. राधा किशन।
Rádhe Kishan	राधे किशन।
Ráe .	. राय।
Ragha .	. रघा।
Raghu-bar	. रघुबर।
Raghu-bír	. रघुबीर।
Raghu-nandan	रघुनन्दन।
Raghu-náth	. रघुनाथ।
Raghu-pat	. रघुपत।
Ráisál .	. राईसाल।

Ráj . राज।
Ráje . राजे।
Ráje Rám . राजे राम।
Rajiwant . रजिवंत।
Ráj-karan . राजकरण।
Ráj-kumár . राजकुमार।
Rájmán . राजमान।
Rajwant . रजवंत।
Rakshpál . रच्छपाल।
Rala . रला।
Rám . राम।
Rámadhín . रामाधीन।
Rámanand . रामानन्द।
Ramanka . रमंका।
Rám-autár . राम औतार। (राम अवतार)।
Rám-bakhsh . रामबखश।
Rám-bali . रामबली।
Rám baran . रामबरण।
Rám basáwan रामबसावन।
Rám bharos . रामभरोस।
Rám-chand . रामचंद।
Rám-chandar . रामचंदर।
Rám-charan . रामचरण।
Rám-charitr . रामचरित्र।
Rám-charittar . रामचरित्तर।
Rám-chhor . रामछोर।
Rám-daiya . रामदैया।
Rám-dás . रामदास।
Rám-datt . रामदत्त।
Rám-datta . रामदत्ता।
Rám-dayál . रामदयाल।
Rám-dhan . रामधन।
Rám-dhári . रामधारी।
Rám-din . रामदीन।
Rám-ditta . रामदित्ता।
Rám-Gopál . रामगोपाल।
Rám-gulám . रामगुलाम।
Rám-harakh . रामहरष।
Rám-het . रामहेत।
Rám-jayáwan रामजयावन।
Rám-jiáwan रामजिआवन।
Rám-ji Lál . रामजी लाल।
Rám-jít . रामजीत।
Ram karan . रामकरण।
Rám-kirat . रामकीरत।
Ram-Kisun . रामकिसुन।
Rám-lagan . रामलगन।
Rám-Lál . रामलाल।
Rám-lauṭan . रामलौटन।
Rám lochan . रामलोचन।
Ramma . रम्मा।
Rammu . रम्मू।
Rám Nand . रामनन्द।
Rám Náráyan रामनारायण।
Rám Náth रामनाथ।
Rám-newáz . रामनेवाज़।
Rám-nídhí . रामनिधी।
Rám padárath . रामपदारथ।
Rám-pargás . रामपरगास।
Rám-parshád . रामपरशाद।
Rám-partáb . रामपरताब।
Rám-phal . रामफल।
Rám-rakkha . रामरक्खा।
Rám-ratan . रामरतन।
Rám-rikh . रामरिख।
Rám ,sabha . रामसभा।
Rám ṣaháe . रामसहाय।

Rám-sajíwan . रामसजीवन ।
Rám-saran . रामसरण ।
Rám-sarúp . रामसरूप ।
Rám-suchet . रामसुचेत ।
Rám-suchit . रामसुचित ।
Rám-sukh . रामसुख ।
Rám-sundar . रामसुंदर ।
Rám-ṭahal . रामटहल ।
Rám-udit . रामउदित ।
Raṇ . . रण ।
Raṇá . . रणा ।
Ran-bahádur . रन बहादुर ।
Ran-bír . रनबीर ।
Ran-dhir . रनधीर ।
Rangi . . रङ्गी ।
Ran-jít . . रनजीत ।
Ran-jor . रनजोर ।
Rarmal . . ररमल ।
Rasíla . . रसीला ।
Ratan . . रतन ।
Rati-bhán . रती भान ।
Rati-pál . . रती पाल ।
Rati Rám . रती राम ।
Ratna . . रतना ।
Richha Rám . रिछा राम ।
Rijandar . रिजंदर ।
Rikhesar . रिखेसर ।
Risál . . रिसाल ।
Rísál . . रीसाल ।
Rohan . . रोहन ।
Rora . . रोड़ा ।
Roshan . रोशन ।
Rudera . रुदेरः ।
Rudr . . रुद्र ।
Rugha . . रुघा ।
Rughnáth . रुघनाथ ।
Rukm . . रुकम ।
Ruldu . . रुल्दू ।
Rúldu . . रूल्दू ।
Ruṇsu . . रूंसू ।
Rúp . . रूप ।
Rúpa . . रूपा ।
Rúpan . . रूपन ।
Rúp-chand . रूपचंद ।
Rúp Rám . रूप राम ।
Rúr . . रूर ।
Ruṛ . . रुड़ ।
Rúra . . रूरा ।
Rúṛa . . रूड़ा ।

H

Sábal . . साबल ।
Sabarjít . . सरबजीत ।
Sábdhán . साबधान ।
Sada . . सदा ।
Sada-phal . सदा फल ।
Sada Rám . सदा राम ।
Sada-sukh . सदा सुख ।
Sádho . . साधो ।
Sádho Rám . साधो राम ।
Sádhu . . साधू ।
Sadoli . . सदोली ।
Ságar . . सागर ।
Sagun . . सगुन ।
Safa . . सफा ।

Saháe .	. सहाय ।
Sahái .	. सहाई ।
Sahaj Rám	. सहज राम ।
Sáheb .	. साहेब ।
Sáheb-dín	. साहेब दीन ।
Sáheb Rám	. साहेब राम ।
Sáhib .	. साहिब ।
Sáhib-dín	. साहिब दीन ।
Sáhib-ditta	. साहिब दित्ता ।
Sahi Rám	. सही राम ।
Sahjáda	. सहजादा ।
Sahtú .	. सहतू ।
Saiḍha .	. सैढा ।
Sajáda .	. सजादा ।
Sakti .	. सकती ।
Sálag .	. सालग ।
Sálagrám	. सालगराम ।
Salámat	. सलामत ।
Saldi .	. सल्दी ।
Sálik .	. सालिक ।
Sálima .	. सालिमा ।
Salku .	. सल्कू ।
Salúkan	. सलूकन ।
Salwant	. सलवंत ।
Sama .	. समा ।
Saman .	. समन ।
Sáman .	. सामन (सांमन) ।
Sámand .	. सामंद ।
Samandar	. समंदर ।
Samant .	. समंत ।
Samman	. संमन ।
Sampat .	. संपत ।
Samud .	. समुद ।
Sandal .	. सन्दल ।

Sangam	. सङ्गम ।
Sánge .	. सांगे ।
Sangrám	. संग्राम ।
Sankal-díp	. संकलदीप ।
Sankar .	. संकर ।
Sankari bakhsh	संकरी बख्श ।
Sankaṭa	. संकटा ।
Sankaṭha	. संकठा ।
Sankru	. संक्रू ।
Sanṣár .	. संसार ।
Sant .	. संत ।
Santi Rám	. संती राम ।
Santok .	. संतोक ।
Santokh	. संतोष ।
Santu .	. संतू ।
Sán̲wal .	. सांवल ।
Sán̲want	. सांवंत ।
Sán̲wat	. सांवत ।
Sarab-dawan	. सरबदवन ।
Sarab-jít	. सरबजीत ।
Sarab-sukh	. सरबसुख ।
Saran .	. सरण ।
Sarani .	सरणी ।
Saranu .	. सरणु ।
Saráfi .	. सराफी ।
Sarb-dayál	. सर्ब दयाल ।
Sarb-sukh	. सर्ब सुख ।
Sarbu .	. सर्बु ।
Sarda .	. सर्दा ।
Sardár .	. सर्दार ।
Sardára	. सर्दारा ।
Sardáru	. सर्दारू ।
Sardha .	. सर्धा ।
Sardul .	. सर्दुल ।

Sardúl .	. सर्दूल।
Sarjít .	. सरजीत।
Sarju .	. सर्जू।
Sarmukh	. सरमुख।
Saudágar	. सौदागर।
Sáukhi .	. साउखी।
Sáula .	. साउला।
Sáun .	. साउन।
Sáwal .	. सावल।
Sáwan .	. सावन।
Sáwan-mal	. सावनमल।
Seḍhu .	. सेढू।
Sera .	. सेरा।
Setusái .	. सेतूसाईं।
Sewa .	. सेवा।
Sewa Rám	. सेवा राम।
Sewak .	. सेवक।
Sewak Lál	. सेवक लाल।
Sewak Rám	. सेवक राम।
Shádi .	. शादी।
Shádi Rám	. शादी राम।
Shálag	. शालग।
Shálígrám	. शालिग्राम।
Shám .	. शाम।
Shámạ .	. शामा।
Shám Náráyan	शाम नारायण।
Shamsher	. शमशेर।
Shangam	. शंगम।
Shankar	. शंकर।
Sharam .	. शरम।
Sheḍa .	. शेडा।
Sheḍu .	. शेडू।
Sher .	. शेर।
Shera .	शेरा।

Sher-jang	. शेरजंग।
Shib .	. शिब।
Shibba .	. शिब्बा।
Shibbu .	. शिब्बू।
Shib-datt	. शिबदत्त।
Shib-karan	. शिबकरन।
Shib-Lál	. शिबलाल।
Shílwant	. शीलवंत।
Shimbhu	. शिंभू।
Shitáb .	. शिताब।
Shiu .	. शिव (शिऊ)।
Shiu-ambar	. शिवअंबर।
Shiu-bálak	. शिवबालक।
Shiu badan	. शिवबदन।
Shiu-bakhsh	. शिवबखश।
Shiu-chand	. शिवचंद।
Shiu-charan	. शिवचरण।
Shiu-darshan	. शिवदर्शन।
Shiu datt	. शिवदत्त।
Shin-dayál	. शिवदयाल।
Shiu dín	. शिवदीन।
Shiu-gulám	. शिवगुलाम।
Shiu-ji .	. शिवजी।
Shiu-karn	. शिवकर्ण।
Shiu-Lál	. शिवलाल।
Shiu-mangal	. शिवमङ्गल।
Shin-nandan	शिवनन्दन।
Shiu Náráyan	शिवनारायण।
Shiu-náth	. शिवनाथ।
Shiu pál	. शिवपाल।
Shiu-parshád	. शिवपरसाद।
Shin-ráj	. शिवराज।
Shiu-rákhan	. शिवराखन।
Shiu Rám	. शिवराम।
Shiu-ratan	. शिवरतन।

Shiu-ságar . शिवसागर ।
Shiu-saháe . शिवसहाय ।
Shiu-sampat . शिवसंपत ।
Shiu-sharan . शिवशरण ।
Shiu shankar . शिवशंकर ।
Shiu-ṭahal . शिवटहल ।
Shri-náth . श्रीनाथ ।
Shukháli . शुखाली ।
Sib . . सिब ।
Síban . सीबन ।
Sibba . . सिब्बा ।
Sibbu . . सिब्बू ।
Si-dayál . सिदयाल ।
Siddhi . . सिद्धी ।
Siddhu . . सिद्धू ।
Si-gulám . सिगुलाम ।
Síha . . सीहा ।
Sihnu . . सिहणू ।
Sí Kishan . सीकिशन ।
Silwant . . सिलवंत ।
Simbhu . . सिंभू ।
Si Náráyan . सी नारायण ।
Singára . सिगारा ।
Singh-man . सिंहमन ।
Singh Rám . सिंह राम ।
Singhu . . सिंघू ।
Sing Rám . सिंग राम ।
Singu . . सिंगू ।
Sirí pat . . सिरीपत ।
Sís Rám . सीस राम ।
Sitáb . . सिताब ।
Sítal . . सीतल ।
Síta Ram . सीता राम ।
Siu-baṇs . सिउबंस ।
Siu baran . सिउबरन ।
Siu-bhankar . सिउभंकर ।
Siu-dán . सिउदान ।
Siu-Hari-dam सिउहरिदम ।
Siu-náth . सिउनाथ ।
Siu-pál . . सिउपाल ।
Siu-pál Rám . सिउपाल राम ।
Siu Rám . सिउराम ।
Siu-rattan . सिउरत्तन ।
Siu-saran . सिउसरन ।
Siu-ṭahal . सिउटहल ।
Sobha . . सोभा ।
Sobha Rám . सोभा राम ।
Sohan . . सोहन ।
Sohanu . सोहनू (सोहणू) ।
Soliya . . सोलिया ।
Srí Kishn . स्री किशन ।
Srí Krishn . स्री कृष्ण ।
Srí pál . . स्री पाल ।
Srí pat . . स्री पत ।
Srí Rám . स्री राम ।
Suambar . सुअंबर ।
Súba . . सूबा ।
Subba . . सुब्बा ।
Subbu . . सुब्बू ।
Subdhán . सुबधान ।
Subhaí . . सुभई ।
Subh-karan . सुभकरन ।
Sucha . . सुचा ।
Suchet . . सुचेत ।
Suebeta . सुचेता ।
Suchit . . सुचित ।
Súḍa . . सूडा ।
Sudágar . सुदागर ।
Sudáma . सुदामा ।

Sudar . . सुदर । *
Suddhu . . सुडू ।
Sudh . . सुध ।
Sudha . . सुधा ।
Súghaṛ . . सूघड़ ।
Sugríb . . सुग्रीब ।
Suháwa . . सुहावा ।
Suhel . . सुहेल ।
Suján . . सुजान ।
Sukha . . सुखा ।
Sukhaí . . सुखई ।
Sukh-chain . सुखचैन ।
Sukh-dayál . सुखदयाल ।
Sukh-deo . सुखदेव ।
Sukh-dhán . सुखधान ।
Sukh-Lál . सुखलाल ।
Sukh-mangal . सुखमङ्गल ।
Sukh-nandan . सुखनन्दन ।
Sukh-ráj . सुखराज ।
Sukh Rám . सुखराम ।
Sukh-ran . सुखरन ।
Sukhu . . सुखू ।
Su lakhan सुलषन ।
Sultáni . . सुल्तानी ।
Sumer . . सुमेर ।
Sumund . सुमुंद ।
Sunág . . सुनाग ।
Sundar . . सुंदर ।
Suphal . . सुफल ।
Suphal Rám . सुफल राम ।
Súr . . सूर ।
Súraj-bakhsh . सूरज बखश ।
Súraj-bali . सूरज बली ।
Súraj-pál . सूरज पाल ।
Súraj-parshád सूरज परशाद ।
Surat (Súrat) . सुरत (सूरत) ।
Súrat bhán . सूरत भान ।
Súrat Rám . सूरत राम ।
Surâyan . सुरायण ।
Surâyán . सुरायाण ।
Surja . . सुर्जा ।
Surjan . . सुर्जन ।
Surj-pál . सुर्जपाल ।
Surju . . सुर्जू ।
Súrmak . . सूरमक ।
Surmakh . सुरमख ।
Suthra . . सुथ्रा ।
Syálu . . स्यालू ।
Syám . . स्याम ।
Syáma . . स्यामा ।
Syám Bihári . स्याम बिहारी ।
Swámi Náráyan स्वामी नारायण ।
Swarúp . स्वरूप ।

T

Ṭahal . . टहल ।
Tahdil . . तहदिल ।
Ṭahil . . टहिल ।
Ṭail . . टैल ।
Ṭanḍa . . टण्डा ।
Tára . . तारा ।

* Perhaps a mis-spelling of Sundar सुंदर .

Tára-chand	. ताराचंद ।
Taríf .	. तरीफ ।
Tarlok .	. तरलोक ।
Ṭeḍu .	. टेडू ।
Tej .	. तेज ।
Teja .	. तेजा ।
Tej-Rám	. तेजराम ।
Ṭek .	. टेक ।
Ṭek Rám	. टेकराम ।
Thahalli	. थहल्लो ।
Ṭhákur .	. ठाकुर ।
Ṭhákur-dás	. ठाकुर दास ।
Ṭhákur-dín	. ठाकुर दीन ।
Ṭhakuri .	. ठकुरो ।
Ṭhákuru .	. ठाकुरू ।
Thamman	. थम्मन (थंमन) ।
Ṭhebu .	. ठेबू ।
Ṭhem Rám	. ठेम राम ।
Thola .	. थोला ।
Tholu .	. थोलू ।
Thor .	. थोर ।
Thúman	. थूमन ।
Thummu	. थुम्मू ।
Ṭhuniyáṉ	. ठुणियां ।
Ṭíka .	. टीका ।
Ṭíka Rám	. टीका राम ।
Ṭíkam .	. टीकम ।
Tikhu .	. तिखू ।
Tilak .	. तिलक ।
Tilak dhari	. तिलक धारी ।
Tilok .	. तिलोक ।
Tiloka .	. तिलोका ।
Ṭoḍa .	. टोडा ।
Tofa* .	. तोफा ।
Tofa-Ram	. तोफा राम ।
Ṭollu .	. टोल्लू ।
Torab .	. तोरब ।
Tota .	. तोता ।
Tota Ram	. तोता राम ।
Toti .	. तोती ।
Totta .	. तोत्ता ।
Tribeni-pál	. त्रिबेनी पाल ।
Tri-bhuwan	. त्रिभुवन ।
Triloka	. त्रिलोका ।
Tuhiya .	. तुहिया ।
Tula Rám	. तुला राम ।
Tulja Rám	. तुल्जा राम ।
Tulsa .	. तुलसा ।
Tulsi .	. तुलसो ।
Tulsi Rám	. तुलसी राम ।
Ṭunḍa .	. टुण्डा ।
Ṭúndar .	टूंदर ।
Turanti .	. तुरंतो ।
Turti .	. तुरतो ।
Tusa .	. तुसा ।

U

Uchit .	. उचित ।
Udai Uday	. ऊदै ऊदय ।
Uday-Rám	. ऊदय राम ।
Udam .	. ऊदम ।

* For Arabic Tuhfa.

Údan . . ऊदन ।
Ude . . उदे ।
Údham . . ऊधम ।
Údho . . ऊधो ।
Udit . . उदित ।
Uditt . . उदित्त ।
Udmi . . उदमी ।
Udmín . . उदमीं ।
Udmí Rám . उदमी राम ।
Udyam . . उद्यम ।
Ugi . . उगी ।
Ugrah Naráyan उग्रह नरायण ।
Ujágar . . उजागर ।
Ujjal . उज्जल ।
Uma-datt . उमा दत्त ।
Umán . . उमां ।
Úmar . . ऊमर ।
Umed . . उमेद ।
Umeg . . उमेग ।
Ummed . उम्मेद ।
Umráo . . उम्राओ (उमराव) ।
Unok . . उनोक ।
Utam . . उतम ।
Uttam . . उत्तम ।

W

Wadháwa . वधावा ।
Wakil . . वकील ।
Wazir . . वज़ीर ।
Wazíra . . वज़ीरा ।
Wazíru . . वज़ीरू ।

Y

Yádu Rám . यादु राम ।
Yád Rám . याद राम ।
Yánnu . . यांनू ।
Yodha . . योधा ।
Yogu . . योगू ।

Z

Zabra . . ज़बरा ।
Záhir . . ज़ाहिर ।
Zálim . ज़ालिम ।
Zauki Rám . ज़ौकी राम ।
Zoráwar . ज़ोरावर ।

APPENDIX TO LIST OF HINDU NAMES.

[*N.B.*—For the reasons given in paragraph 2 of the Introduction, the following list of castes and clans is far from complete; at best it represents only the names found in the Bengal Army, and under Rájpút clans, only a very few of these. The names given in brackets are duplicate or alternative spellings of the unbracketed names which they follow.]

Hindu Castes.

Áhar	आहर।
Ahír	अहीर।
Baheliya	बहेलिया।
Baniya	बनिया।
Bári	बारी।
Beṛiya	बेड़िया।
Bháṭ	भाट।
Bhunjwa	भुंजवा।
[Bhujwa	भुजवा।]
Bráhman	ब्राह्मन।
Chamár	चमार।
Chíng	चींग।
Chhípa	छीपा।
Dhánukh	धानुख।
[Dhánuk	धानुक।]
Ḍogra	डोग्रा।
Gareṛiya	गरेड़िया।
[Garaṛiya	गरड़िया।]
Gosáiṇ	गोसाईं।
Gújar	गूजर।
Halwái	हलवाई।
Jáṭ	जाट।
Jaṭṭ	जट्ट।
Kábu	काबु।
Káchhi	काछी।
Kahár	कहार।
Kalár	कलार।
[Kalwár	कल्वार।]
Kanait	कनैत।
Káyath	कायथ।
[Káyasth	कायस्थ।]
Khatri	खत्री।
Kumhár	कुम्हार।
Kúri	कूरी।
Kurmi	कुर्मी।
Lawáni	लवानी।
Lodh	लोध।
Lohár	लोहार।
Luára	लुआरा।
Mahto	महतो।
[Mahetoṇ	महेतों।]
[Maito	मयतो।]
Manár	मनार।
Mania	मनिया।
Mehtar	मेहतर।
Muraí	मुरई।
[Murái	मुराई।]
Nái	नाई।
[Náu	नाऊ।]
Pási	पासी।
Rájpút	राजपूत।
Saini	सैनी।
Sikh	सिख।
Sonár	सोनार।
[Sunár	सुनार।]
Tamoli	तमोली।

Titles of Brahmans.

Agniho	अग्निहोत्री ।	Ojha	ओझा ।
Awasthi	अवस्थी ।	Páṉṛe	पांड़े ।
	बाजपेई ।	[Pánḍe	पांडे ।]
Chaube	चौबे ।	Páṭhak	पाठक ।
Dichhit	दिछित ।	Sukul	सुकुल ।
[Dikshit	दिच्चित ।]	Tiwári	तिवारी ।
Dube	दुबे ।	Tribedi	त्रिबेदी ।
[Dúbe	दूबे ।]	Upádhya	उपाध्या ।
Misir	मिसिर ।	[Upadhya	उपध्या ।]
[Misr	मिश्र ।]		

Clans of Rájpúts.

Bachgoti	बचगोती ।	Gargbaṉsi	गर्गबंसी ।
Bais	बैस ।	Gaur	गौर ।
Bandalgoti	बंदलगोती ।	Gautam	गौतम ।
Bhadauriya	भदौरिया ।	Junwár	जुनवार ।
Bhálesultán	भालेसुलतान ।	Kachwáha	कछवाहा ।
Bisen	बिसेन ।	Kanpuriya	कनपुरिया ।
Chauhán	चौहान ।	Pawár	पवार ।
Durgbaṉsi	दुर्गबंसी ।	Sombaṉsi	सोमबंसी ।

Gurkháli Castes.

Adhikári	अधिकारी ।	Jaisi	जैसी ।
Ále	आले ।	Kárki	कार्की ।
Bhanḍári	भंडारी ।	Kawar	कवर ।
Bishṭ	बीष्ट ।	Kharka	खड़का ।
Buṛathoki	बुड़ाथोकी ।	Khattri	खत्री ।
Damái	दमाई ।	Khawás	खवास ।
Dura	दुरा ।	Láma	लामा ।
Ghale	घले ।	Magar	मगर ।
Gharti	घर्ती ।	Mahat	महत ।
Gurúng	गुड़ूं ।	Mal	मल ।
[Gurúm	गुरूम ।]	Nagarkoti	नगरकोटी ।
Hamál	हमाल ।	Newár	नेवार ।

Gurkháli Castes—concld.

Pun .	. पुण ।	Sáhi .	. साह्री ।
Ráe .	. राय ।	Sain .	. सैन ।
Rána .	. राणा ।	Sárki .	. सार्की ।
Ráwal .	. राव्ल ।	Singh .	. सिंह ।
Roka .	. रोका ।	Thápa .	. थापा ।

NAMES OF MUHAMMADANS

A

Ábád . .	آباد
Abban . .	ابّن
'Abbás	عبّاس
'Abbás 'Ali .	عبّاس علي
'Abbás Husain .	عباس حسين
'Abdul . .	عبدل
'Abdul-Ahad .	عبدالاحد
'Abdul-Ghafúr	عبدالغفور
'Abdul-Ghani .	عبدالغني
'Abdul-Halím .	عبدالحليم
'Abdul-Husain .	عبدالحسين
'Abdul-Karím .	عبدالكريم
'Abdul-Khálik .	عبدالخالق
'Abdullah .	عبدالله
'Abdullah Núr	عبدالله نور
'Abdul-Latíf	عبداللطيف
'Abdul-Majíd .	عبدالمجيد
'Abdul-Wáhid .	عبدالواحد
'Abdur-Rahím .	عبدالرحيم
'Abd-r-Rahmán	عبدالرحمن
'Abdur-Rashíd	عبدالرشيد
'Abdus-Salám .	عبدالسلام
'Abdus Samad .	عبدالصمد
Ádam . .	آدم
Aggu . .	اگّو
Ágha . .	آغا
Afzal . .	افضل
Ahmad . .	احمد
Ahmad 'Ali .	احمد علي
Ahmad-bakhsh	احمد بخش
Ahmad-dín .	احمد دين
Ahmad Gul .	احمد گل
Ahmad Sháh .	احمد شاه
Ahmad Sher .	احمد شير
Ahmad-yár .	احمد يار
'Ajab . .	عجب
Ajmeri . .	اجميري
Akbar . .	اكبر
Akbar Ali .	اكبر علي
Akbar Husain .	اكبر حسين
Akhtar . .	اختر
Akhtar Sháh .	اختر شاه
Alah-bakhsh .	اله بخش
Alah-dín .	اله دين
Alah ditta .	اله دتّا
Alah-rakkha .	اله ركّها
Alah-yár .	اله يار
'Álam . .	عالم
'Álam 'Alí .	عالم علي
'Alamdár Husain .	علمدار حسين
'Alam-din .	علم دين
'Alam sher .	عالم شير
'Aláud-dín .	علاءالدين
'Aláwal .	علاول
'Ali . .	علي
'Ali bahádur .	علي بهادر
'Ali-bakhsh .	علي بخش
'Ali-dád . .	علي داد
Alif . .	الف

Alíf	اليف
'Ali Husain	علي حسين
'Alím	عليم
'Ali Mardán	علي مردان
'Ali Muhammad	علي محمد
'Ali Murád	علي مراد
'Alíud-dín	علي‌الدين
Allah-ditta	الله دتا
Allah Núr	الله نور
Altáf Husain	الطاف حسين
Amán 'Ali	امان علي
Amánat	امانت
Amánat 'Ali	امانت علي
Amánullah	امان‌الله
Amín	امين
Amínud-daula	امين‌الدوله
Amír	امير
Amír 'Ali	امير علي
Amír-dád	امير داد
Amjad	امجد
Amjad 'Ali	امجد علي
Anwar	انور
A'rab	عرب
Árif 'Ali	عارف علي
Arsla	ارسله , ارسلا
Asad 'Ali	اسد علي
Asadullah	اسدالله
Ásaf	آصف
Ásaf 'Ali	آصف علي
Asghar	اصغر
Asghar Husain	اصغر حسين
'Áshik 'Ali	عاشق علي
'Ashik Muham-mad	عاشق محمد
Ashnáki	اشناكي
Ashraf	اشرف
Aslam	اسلم
'Atáe Muham-mad	عطاى محمد
'Ata Husain	عطا حسين
'Ata Muham-mad	عطا محمد
'Atar	عطر
'Atáullah	عطاالله
'Aulád Husain	اولاد حسين
Auliya	اوليا
Ausán	اوسان
Ayya	ايا
Ázád	آزاد
A'zam	اعظم
A'zam 'Ali	اعظم علي
'Azim	عظيم
'Azím-bakhsh	عظيم بخش
'Azíz	عزيز
'Aziz 'Ali	عزيز علي
'Azízud-dín	عزيزالدين
'Azmat	عظمت
'Azmatullah	عظمت‌الله

B

Bába	بابا
Bába-ján	بابا جان
Bachu	بچو
Badal	بدل
Bádal	بادل
Badr-dín	بدر دين

Badrud-dín	بدرالدين
Báḍu	باڈو
Bádullah	بادالله
Bágh 'Ali	باغ علي
Baghi	بگهي
Bágu	باگو
Bahádur	بهادر
Bahádur 'Ali	بهادر علي
Bahádur-Sher	بهادر شير
Baháud-din	بهاء الدين
Baháwal	بهاول
Baháwal-bakhsh	بهاول بخش
Bahrám	بهرام
Bairi	بيري
Bak	بك
Bakhshan	بخشن
Bakhshish	بخشش
Bakhshish 'Ali	بخشش علي
Bakhtáwar	بختاور
Báḳir 'Ali	باقر علي
Bakka	بكّا
Bála-dín	بالادين
Banán	بنان
Banda-e 'Ali	بندۀ علي
Band i 'Ali	بندِ علي
Báṉka	بانكا
Bári	باري
Barkat 'Ali	بركت علي
Bar-khurdár	برخوردار
Baryám	بريام
Basáwan	بساون
Bashárat	بشارت
Bashárat 'Ali	بشارت علي
Báz	باز
Báz gul	بازگل
Bázíd	بازيد
Báz-núr	بازنور
Báz Muhammad	باز محمد
Beche	بيچے
Bhág	بهاگ
Bhaggu	بهگو
Bhikkha	بهكّها
Bhola	بهولا
Bhole	بهولے
Bhúre	بهورے
Bihári	بهاري
Biloch	بلوچ
Boṛa	بوڑا
Bostán	بوستان
Bú-'Ali-bakhsh	بوعلي بخش
Buddhu	بدّهو
Buḍḍhan	بڈّهن
Budhu	بدهو
Buláki	بلاقي
Buland	بلند
Bunyád	بنياد
Burhán-dín	برهان دين
Búṭa	بوٹا

C

Chánd	چاند
Chandan	چندن
Chaughaṭṭa	چوگهٹّا
Chhannu	چهنّو

Chhedi	چهيدي
Chirágh	چراغ
Chirágh 'Ali	چراغ علي
Chirágh-dín	چراغ دين
Chirághud-dín	چراغ الدين

D

Dád-gul	داد گل
Dád-sher	داد شير
Dáḍu	داڈو
Dáim 'Ali	دائم علي
Dalel	دليل
Dalmír	دلمير
Daráz	دراز
Daráz Muhammad	دراز محمد
Dargáhi	درگاهي
Daríra	دريره
Dar-Muhammad	درمحمد
Darweza	درويزه
Dasaundhe	دسوندهے
Dáúd	داؤد
Daulat	دولت
Didár	ديدار
Diláwar	دلاور
Dildár	دلدار
Dil Muhammad	دل محمد
Dín Muhammad	دين محمد
Dítta	دِتا
Díwán 'Ali	ديوان علي
Dost Muhammad	دوست محمد
Dúlu	دولو
Dúnde	دوندے

F

Fahmi	فهمي
Faiz	فيض
Faiz Muhammad	فيض محمد
Faḳíra	فقيرا
Fakír-bakhsh	فقير بخش
Fakír Muhammad	فقير محمد
Faḳír Sháh	فقير شاه
Faḳír Yahya	فقير يحيي
Farangi	فرنگي
Farhat Husain	فرحت حسين
Faríd	فريد
Farmán	فرمان
Farmán 'Ali	فرمان علي
Farzand 'Ali	فرزند علي
Fasíhullah	فصيح الله
Fateh-dín	فتح دين
Fateh-jang	فتح جنگ
Fateh Muhammad	فتح محمد
Fathud-dín	فتح الدين
Faujdár	فوجدار
Fauji	فوجي

Faiyáz 'Ali	فياض علي
Fázil	فاضل
Fazl	فضل
Fazl 'Ali	فضل علي
Fazl-dád	فضل داد
Fazl Haḳḳ	فضل حق
Fazl Sháh	فضل شاه
Firoz	فيروز

G

Gahli	گهلي
Gáhu	گاهو
Gámi	گامي
Gasíṭa	گسيٹه
Gauhar	گوهر
Gauhar 'Ali	گوهر علي
Ghaffár	غفّار
Ghafúr	غفور
Ghálib 'Ali	غالب علي
Ghási	گهاسي
Ghaus Muhammad	غوث محمد
Ghazan	غزن
Ghazanfar 'Ali	غضنفر علي
Gházi	غازي
Gházi-bakhsh	غازي بخش
Gháziud-din*	غازي الدين
Ghirráu	گهرّاؤ
Ghulám	غلام
Ghulám 'Abbás	غلام عباس
Ghulám 'Ali	غلام علي
Ghulám Haidar	غلام حيدر
Ghulám Hasan	غلام حسن
Ghulám Hazrat	غلام حضرت
Ghulám Husain	غلام حسين
Ghulám Jáfar	غلام جعفر
Ghulám Kásim	غلام قاسم
Ghulám Muhammad	غلام محمد
Ghulám Muhiyuddín†	غلام محي الدين
Ghulám Murtaza	غلام مرتضى
Ghulám Mustafa	غلام مصطفى
Ghulám Nabi	غلام نبي
Ghulám Rasúl	غلام رسول
Ghulám Siddík	غلام صدّيق
Goḍar	گوڈر
Golaí	گولئي
Golín	گولين
Gujjar	گجّر
Gul	گل
Guláb	گلاب
Gul Akhmand	گل اخمند
Gul-daráz	گل دراز
Gul Halim	گل حليم
Gul Hasan	گل حسن
Gulistán	گلستان
Gul Muhammad	گل محمد
Gul Sháh	گل شاه
Gulzár	گلزار
Gulzár Husain	گلزار حسين

* This is the ordinary Indian pronunciation The correct vocalization is *Gházid-dín*
† This also is the popular pronunciation, instead of the correct *Muhyiddín*

H

Habíb	حبيب
Habíb 'Ali	حبيب علي
Habíbullah	حبيب‌الله
Habíbur-Rahmán	حبيب الرحمن
Hádi yár	هادي يار
Háfiz 'Ali	حافظ علي
Hafízullah	حفيظ‌الله
Haidar	حيدر
Haidar 'Ali	حيدر علي
Haidar-bakhsh	حيدر بخش
Háji	حاجي
Hakdád	حق‌داد
Hákim	حاكم
Hak-nawáz	حق نواز
Háku	هاكو
Halím	حليم
Hamd	حمد
Hámid	حامد
Hamíd	حميد
Haríf Gul	حريف گل
Háṛu	هاڑو
Hasan	حسن
Hasan Raza*	حسن رضا
Háshim 'Ali	هاشم علي
Hassu	حسو
Háthi	هاتهي
Hayát	حيات
Hayát Ahmad	حيات احمد
Hayát 'Ali	حيات علي
Hayát bakhsh	حيات بخش
Hayát Gul	حيات گل
Ḥayát Muhammad	حيات محمد
Hayátullah	حيات‌الله
Hazabr	هزبر
Hazrat	حضرت
Hetu	هيتو
Hiḍáyat	هدايت
Hidáyat 'Ali	هدايت علي
Hikmat	حكمت
Himáyatullah	حمايت‌الله
Himmat	همّت
Híra	هيرا
Híre	هيرے
Hoshyár 'Ali	هوشيار علي
Hubdár	حبدار
Hurmat	حرمت
Hurmat 'Ali	حرمت علي
Husain	حسين
Hussain 'Ali	حسين علي
Husain-bakhsh	حسين بخش
Husámud-din	حُسام‌الدين

I

Ibráhím	ابراهيم
Ibráhím 'Ali	ابراهيم علي
'Íd-bakhsh	عيد بخش
Iftikhár Husain	افتخار حسين

* Thus pronounced in India: properly *Riza*.

Ihsán . .	احسان
Ihsán 'Ali .	احسان علي
Ikhtiyár . .	اختيار
Ilah bakhsh .	اله بخش
Ilah-dád . .	اله داد
Iláhi . .	الهي
Iláhi-bakhsh .	الهي بخش
Imám . .	امام
Imám 'Ali .	امام علي
Imám-bakhsh .	امام بخش
Imdád . .	امداد
Imdád 'Ali .	امداد علي
'Imrán . .	عِمران
Imroz . .	اِمروز
Imtiyáz Husain	اِمتياز حسين
'Ináyat . .	عنايت
'Ináyat 'Ali .	عنايت علي
'Ináyat Husain	عنايت حسين
Irshád 'Ali .	ارشاد علي
'Ísa . .	عيسى
Ísfandiyár .	اسفنديار
Islám . .	اسلام
Islám 'Ali .	اسلام علي
Isma'íl . .	اسمٰعيل
'Ismatullah .	عصمت‌الله
'Iyárud-dín .	عيارالدين
'Izzat . .	عزت

J

Jabar . .	جبر
Jáfar . .	جعفر
Jáfar 'Ali .	جعفر علي
Jahán . .	جهان
Jahángír .	جهانگير
Jahángír 'Ali .	جهانگير علي
Jahángír-bakhsh	جهانگير بخش
Jalálud-dín .	جلال‌الدين
Jallád . .	جلّاد
Jamadár .	جمعدار
Jamál . .	جمال
Jamálud-din .	جمال‌الدين
Jamíl-Ahmad .	جميل احمد
Jánan . .	جانن
Jánas* . .	جانس
Jang-báz .	جنگ باز
Jangi . .	جنگي
Jang-sher .	جنگشير
Ján Muhammad	جان محمد
Jaralla . .	جرلّا
Jauhar 'Ali .	جوهر علي
Jawáb . .	جواب
Jawáhir . .	جواهر
Jawáhira .	جواهرا
Jhajju . .	جهجّو
Jhande . .	جهنڈے
Jhandi Sháh .	جهنڈي شاه
Jharí . .	جهري
Jíbi . .	جيبي
Jítan . .	جيتن
Jíte . .	جيتے
Jíu . .	جيو

* Perhaps the name of a Eurasian,—Johns (?)

Jíwan . .	جیون	Jumman .	جُمّن
Juma . .	جمعه	Jundi . .	جُندي
Juman . .	جُمن		

K

Ḳabúl . .	قبول	Káshif 'Ali .	کاشف علي
Ḳadír . .	قدير	Kashmír .	کشمير
Ḳádir . .	قادر	Kashmíri .	کشميري
Ḳádir 'Ali .	قادر علي	Kásím . .	قاسم
Ḳádir-dád .	قادر داد	Ḳásim 'Ali .	قاسم علي
Ḳáim . .	قائم	Ḳásim-dín .	قاسم دين
Ḳáim 'Ali .	قائم علي	Ḳaṭṭu . .	کٹو
Ḳáim Husain .	قائم حسين	Kázim 'Ali .	کاظم علي
Kajír . .	کجير	Kesar . .	کيسر
Kála . .	کاله	Khádim 'Ali .	خادم علي
Kalandar .	قلندر	Khairát 'Ali .	خيرات علي
Kále . .	کالے	Khairáti .	خيراتي
Kálu . .	کالو	Khair Muhammad . .	خير محمد
Kamál . .	کمال	Khairullah .	خيرالله
Kamála . .	کمالا	Khálik-dád .	خالق داد
Kamál-dín .	کمال دين	Khána . .	خانا
Ḳamarud-dín .	قمرالدين	Kháṉ Bahádur	خان بهادر
Kapúr . .	کپور	Kháni-zamáṉ .	خان زمان
Karam . .	کرم	Khanjar .	خنجر
Karam 'Ali .	کرم علي	Kháṉ Mir .	خان مير
Karámat .	کرامت	Kháṉ Muhammad . .	خان محمد
Karámat 'Ali .	کرامت علي	Khátim 'Ali .	خاتم علي
Karámatullah .	کرامت الله	Khátir-jama .	خاطر جمع
Karam-bakhsh	کرم بخش	Khawáss .	خواصّ
Karím . .	کريم	Khewa . .	کهيوا
Karím 'Ali .	کريم علي	Khewan . .	کهيون
Karím-bakhsh .	کريم بخش		
Karím-dád .	کريم داد		

Khizr-dád	خضرداد
Khoju	خوجو
Khuda-bakhsh	خدا بخش
Khuda-dost	خدا دوست
Khuda-mihr	خدا مهر
Khudáwand	خداوند
Khuda-yár	خدا يار
Khwája-bakhsh	خواجه بخش
Khwája Muhammad	خواجه محمد
Khwáj-bakhsh	خواج بخش
Kifáyat 'Ali	كفايت علي
Ḳiyámud-dín	قيام الدين
Ḳudrat	قدرت
Ḳudrat 'Ali	قدرت علي
Kulwant	كُلونت
Ḳurbán 'Ali	قربان علي
Kúrd	كورد
Kúṛu	كوڑو
Ḳutb	قطب
Ḳutbud-dín	قطب الدين

L

Láik Ali	لائق علي
Lál	لعل , لال
Lála	لاله
Lál-báz	لعل باز
Lál-beg	لعل بيگ
Lál-gul	لعل گل
Lál-mír	لعل مير
Lúl Muhammad	لعل محمد
Langar	لنگر
Latíf	لطيف
Lutf 'Ali	لطف علي
Lutf Sháh	لطف شاه
Lutfullah	لطف الله

M

Madad	مدد
Madad 'Ali	مدد علي
Madah	مدح
Madár	مدار
Madár-bakhsh	مدار بخش
Madat	مدت
Mad-gul	مد گل
Mahbúbullah	محبوب الله
Mahfúz 'Ali	محفوظ علي
Mahmúd	محمود
Mahtáb	مهتاب
Mahtu	مهتو
Majíd	مجيد
Makhdúm	مخدوم
Makhdúm-bakhsh	مخدوم بخش
Mákhe	ماكهے
Makka 'Ali	مكه علي
Malang	ملنگ
Malik	ملك
Malik Muhammad	ملك محمد
Malik Sháh	ملك شاه
Malúk	ملوك

Mámún	مامون
Mána	مانا
Mansab 'Ali	منصب علي
Mansullah	منس الله
Mansúr	منصور
Mansúr 'Ali	منصور علي
Má-shá-allah	ماشاء الله
Mashíyat 'Ali	مشيت علي
Mashíyat Husain	مشيت حسين
Masta	مستا
Matlúb Husain	مطلوب حسين
Maula	مولا
Maula-bakhsh	مولا بخش
Maula-dád	مولا داد
Mausam	موسم
Mausam 'Ali	موسم علي
Mazhar 'Ali	مظهر علي
Mazraí*	مزرئي
Megal	ميگل
Meṛaí	ميڑئي
Mihr	مهر
Mihráb	محراب
Mihráb-din	محراب دين
Mihr 'Ali	مهر علي
Mihr bakhsh	مهر بخش
Mihrbán	مهربان
Mihr-dád	مهر داد
Mihr-iḳlím	مهر اقليم
Mihr Muhammad	مهر محمد
Mihr Sháh	مهر شاه
Minhájud-dín	منهاج الدين
Mír 'Abbás	مير عباس
Mír Afghán	مير افغان
Mír Akhmand	ميراخمند
Mír Álam	مير عالم
Mír 'Ali	مير علي
Míran	ميرن
Míráṉ-bakhsh	ميران بخش
Mír Aslam	مير اسلم
Mír Ghulám	مير غلام
Mír Gul	مير گل
Mir Hasan	مير حسن
Mír Muhammad	مير محمد
Mír Zamáṉ	مير زمان
Misri	مصري
Misru	مسرو
Miyáṉ	ميان
Miyáṉ Gul	ميان گل
Miyáṉ Ján	ميان جان
Moháṅa	موهانه
Mu'azzam	معظم
Mubárak	مبارك
Mubín	مبين
Mughli	مغلي
Muhabbat†	محبت
Muhabbatullah	محبت الله
Muhmadí	محمدي
Muhammad	محمد
Muhammad Afzal	محمد افضل
Muhammad Ahsan	محمد احسن

* Possibly an error of transcription for Mirzai, مرزئي

† Thus always pronounced in India: correctly *Mahabbat.*

Muhammad Akbar .	محمد اكبر
Muhammad Akram . .	محمد اكرم
Muhammad Álam . .	محمد عالم
Muhammad 'Ali . .	محمد علي
Muhammad Asad . .	محمد اسد
Muhammad Asghar .	محمد اصغر
Muhammad Áshúr . .	محمد عاشور
Muhammad A'zam . .	محمد اعظم
Muhammad 'Azím . .	محمد عظيم
Muhammad-bakhsh . .	محمد بخش
Muhammad-dín	محمد دين
Muhammad Ghaus . .	محمد غوث
Muhammad Hasan .	محمد حسن
Muhammad Husain .	محمد حسين
Muhammad Is-hák . .	محمد اسحٰق
Muhammad Isma'il . .	محمد اسمٰعيل
Muhammad Ján	محمد جان
Muhammad Kázim .	محمد كاظم
Muhammad Mahdi . .	محمد مهدي
Muhammad Na'ím . .	محمد نعيم

Muhammad-nawáz . .	محمد نواز
Muhammad Názir . .	محمد ناظر
Muhammad Núr	محمد نور
Muhammad Raza . .	محمد رضا
Muhammad Sadík . .	محمد صديق
Muhammad Sáhib . .	محمد صاحب
Muhammad Sarafráz .	محمد سرافراز
Muhammad Sháh . .	محمد شاه
Muhammad Sher . .	محمد شير
Muhammad Shifá'at .	محمد شفاعت
Muhammad ud-dín .	محمدالدين
Muhammad 'Usmán .	محمد عثمان
Muhammad Yakúb .	محمد يعقوب
Muhammad-yár . .	محمد يار
Muhammad Yúsuf . .	محمد يوسف
Muhammad Zamán . .	محمد زمان
Muhibb 'Ali .	محبّ علي
Muhít . .	محيط
Muhkam-dín .	محكم دين
Muhsin . .	محسن
Mu'in . .	معين
Mu'izz 'Ali .	معزعلي
Mu'izzud-dín .	معزالدين

Mu'izzullah .	معزالله
Mukarrab .	مقرب
Mukarrab Husain .	مقرب حسين
Mukhtár . .	مختار
Mumín* . .	ممين
Mumtáz 'Ali .	ممتاز علي
Munawwar .	منور
Munawwar 'Ali	منوّر علي
Munίd† . .	منيد
Munír . .	منير
Munna . .	مُنّا
Murád . .	مراد
Murád Ali .	مراد علي
Murád-bakhsh .	مراد بخش
Muríd . .	مريد
Músa . .	موسى
Musáhib . .	مصاحب
Musáhib 'Ali .	مصاحب علي
Musalli . .	مسلّي
Musharraf .	مشرّف
Muslim . .	مسلم
Mustafa . .	مصطفى
Mustu . .	مُستو
Muzaffar Husain	مظفر حسين

N

Nabát . .	نبات
Nabi-bakhsh .	نبي بخش
Nádir . .	نادر
Nádir 'Ali . .	نادرعلي
Na'ím . .	نعيم
Na'ím Gul .	نعيم گل
Najaf . .	نجف
Najaf 'Ali .	نجف علي
Najíb . .	نجيب
Najíf‡ . .	نجيف
Najmud-dín .	نجم الدين
Najmul-Islám .	نجم الاسلام
Nakshband .	نقشبند
Námdár . .	نامدار
Nának . .	نانک
Nanhu . .	ننهو
Nasír . .	نصير
Násir . .	ناصر
Násir 'Ali .	ناصرعلي
Nasím Gul .	نسيم گل
Nathe . .	نتهي
Naurang . .	نورنگ
Nawáb . .	نواب
Nawáb Shah .	نواب شاه
Nawáz 'Ali .	نواز علي
Nawázish 'Ali .	نوازش علي
Nazar 'Ali .	نذر علي
Nazar Muhammad . .	نظر محمد
Nazír . .	نظير

---

* A meaningless word, perhaps a mistake for مؤمن Múmin.

† Meaningless, perhaps meant for منير Munír.

‡ Probably a mistake for Najaf نجف or Najib نجيب. Najíf means "a broad-headed arrow," and is hardly likely to be used as a proper name.

Nazír Gul .	نظیر گل
Nazír Husain .	نظیر حسین
Názir Husain .	ناظر حسین
Nek Muhammad	نیک محمد
Ni'amat (Niámat)* .	نعمت
Nihál . .	نہال
Niyáz . .	نیاز
Niyáz 'Ali .	نیاز علي
Niyáz Gul .	نیاز گل
Niyáz Muhammad . .	نیاز محمد
Niyáz ullah .	نیازالله
Nizám 'Ali .	نظام علي
Nizámud dín .	نظام‌الدین
Núr . .	نور
Nur Akbar .	نور اکبر
Núr 'Ali .	نور علي
Núr Muhammad . .	نور محمد
Núr Sháh .	نور شاه
Núrud-dín .	نورالدین
Núrul-Hasan .	نورالحسن
Núrullah .	نورالله
Nusrat . .	نصرت

P

Pádsháh .	پادشاه
Pahlu (perhaps Pahlau) .	پلہو
Pahlwán .	پہلوان
Páín . .	پائین
Paind . .	پیند
Palád . .	پلاد
Panáh . .	پناه
Partáb . .	پرتاب
Patang . .	پتنگ
Páyanda Muhammad .	پاینده محمد
Phagu . .	پھگو
Phalan . .	پھلن
Phína . .	پھینا
Pbuman .	پُھمن
Phumbana .	پُھمبنا
Pír . .	پیر
Pírán-ditta .	پیران دتّا
Pír-bakhsh .	پیر بخش
Pír-dád . .	پیرداد
Pír Muhammad	پیر محمد
Píru .	پیرو
Purdil . .	پردل
Pyáre . .	پیارے

R

Rabb nawáz .	رب نواز
Rafí'ud-dín .	رفیع‌الدین
Ráhat 'Alí .	راحت علي
.	رحیم

* Transliterated as pronounced, for Ni'mat.

Rahím-bakhsh . رحیم بخش
Rahím-dád . رحیم داد
Rahímud-dín . رحیم الدین
Rahím-yár . رحیم یار
Rahm . . رحم
Rahm 'Ali . رحم علي
Rahm Iláhi . رحم الٰهي
Rahmán . رحمان
Rahmat . رحمت
Rahmat 'Ali . رحمت علي
Rahmat Sher . رحمت شیر
Rahmatullah . رحمت الله
Raínán . . رئینان
Rájá . . راجه , راجا
Rajab . . رجب
Rajnu . . رجنو
Rájúli . . راجولي
Ramzán . رمضان
Ramzán 'Ali . رمضان علي
Rangín . . رنگین
Ránje . . رانجي
Rasúl . . رسول
Razá 'Ali . رضا علي
Razáwand . رضاوند
Ráz Gul . راز گل
Rogán . . روگان
Roṛa . . روڑا
Roshan . . روشن
Roshan 'Ali . روشن علي
Ruldu . . رلدو
Rustam . . رستم
Rustam 'Ali . رستم علي

S

Sa'ádat . . سعادت
Sa'ádat 'Ali . سعادت علي
Sa'ádatud-dín . سعادت الدین
Sa'ádu . . سعادو
Sábit . . ثابت
Sádiḳ 'Ali . صادق علي
Sádiḳ Muhammad . . صادق محمد
Sadr-dín . صدر دین
Sa'dullah . سعدالله
Safdar . . صفدر
Safdar 'Ali . صفدر علي
Sahbu . . صحبو
Sáhib 'Ali . صاحب علي
Sáhib-dád . صاحب داد
Sáhib-dín . صاحب دین
Sáhib Muhammad . . صاحب محمد
Saida . . سَیدا
Sa'ídullah . سعیدالله
Saif Ali . . سیف علي
Saifullah . سیف الله
Saiyid . . سیّد
Saiyid 'Alam . سید عالم
Saiyid 'Ali . سید علي
Saiyid Gul . سید گل
Saiyid Ján . سید جان
Saiyid Lál . سید لعل
Saiyid Muhammad . . سید محمد

Sakháwat 'Ali	سخاوت علي
Salámat 'Ali	سلامت علي
Sálár-bakhsh	سالار بخش
Samadullah	صمدالله
Samand	سمند
Samundar	سُمندر
Sanái	سنائي
Sar-afráz (or Sarfaráz)	سرافراز
Sar-báz	سرباز
Sar-buland	سربلند
Sardár	سردار
Sar-mast	سرمست
Sar-parast	سرپرست
Sarwar	سرور
Saudágar	سوداگر
Shabráti	شبراتي
Shádi	شادي
Shádmán	شادمان
Shahádat	شهادت
Shahálam*	شهالم
Shah 'Ali	شاه علي
Sháh-báz	شهباز
Sháh-dád	شاه داد
Sháhi	شاهي
Shahín	شهين
Sháh-nawáz	شاه نواز
Shah-nawáz	شهنواز
Sháh-pasand	شاه پسند
Sháh-sawár	شاه سوار
Shah-sawár	شهسوار
Sháh wali	شاه ولي
Shah-wali	شهولي
Shahzád Mír	شهزاد مير
Sháku	شاكو
Shám beg	شام بيگ
Shams-dín	شمس دين
Shamshád 'Ali	شمشاد علي
Shamsher	شمشير
Shamsher 'Ali	شمشير علي
Shamsud-dín	شمس الدين
Sharaf	شرف
Sharaf 'Ali	شرف علي
Sharfa	شرفا
Sher	شير
Shera	شيرا
Sher 'Ali	شير علي
Sher-báz	شير باز
Sher-dád	شير داد
Sher-dil	شير دل
Sher-dum	شير دُم
Sher-jang	شير جنگ
Sher Muhammad	شير محمد
Sher Zamán	شير زمان
Shíbu	شيبو
Shihábud-dín	شهاب الدين
Shírín	شيرين
Siddíḳ	صديق
Sikandar	سكندر
Sikandar bakhsh	سكندر بخش
Síkdár	سيكدار
Sindhi	سندهي
Sindi	سندي

* *Sic.* Probabiy for شاه عالم Shah' Álam.

Sogal . . سوگل
Sone . . سونے
Subhán . . سبحان
Subhán 'Ali . سبحان علي
Suhbat . . صحبت
Suhráb Gul . سهراب گل
Sukha . . سُکها
Súkhan . . سوکهن
Sulaimán (Suleman) . . سليمان
Sultán . . سلطان
Sultán 'Ali . سلطان علي
Sultán Muhammad . . سلطان محمد
Sultán Sa'd (Sád) . . سلطان سعد
Suráb . . سُراب

T

Tafazzul Husain تفضل حسين
Tajammul Husain . تجمل حسين
Taj Muhammad تاج محمد
Tájud-dín . تاج الدين
Tálib 'Ali . طالب علي
Táli'wand . طالعوند
Tálí'war . طالعور
Tasadduḳ Husain . تصدق حسين
Tawangar Husain . تونگر حسين
Tegh 'Ali . تيغ علي
Tíka . . ٹيکا
Tímúr . . تيمور
Turáb . . تراب
Turáb 'Ali . تراب علي
Turra báz . طُرّة باز

U

'Umar . . عمر
'Umar-bakhsh . عمر بخش
'Umarud-dín . عمر الدين
'Umed . . اميد
Umraí . . امرئي
Umráo . . امراو
Umráo 'Ali . امراو علي
Usmán . . عثمان

W

Wáhid . . واحد
Wáhid 'Ali . واحد علي
Wájid 'Ali . واجد علي
Wali-dád . لي داد
Wáris . . وارث
Wáris 'Ali . وارث علي
Wasíyat 'Ali . وصيت علي
Wazír . . وزير

Wazíra . .	وزيرا	Wídán . .	ويدان
Wazír Muhammad . .	وزير محمد	Wiláyat . .	ولايت
Wazírud-din .	وزير الدين	Wiláyat 'Ali .	ولايت علي
		Wiláyat-Husain	ولايت حسين

Y

Yád 'Ali .	ياد علي	Yár Muhammad	يار محمد
Yad-i-A'zam .	يد اعظم	Yá-sín . .	ياسين
Yáḳúb 'Ali .	يعقوب علي	Yatím . .	يتيم
Yáran . .	يارن	Yúsuf 'Ali .	يوسف علي
Yár Gul . .	يار گل		

Z

Zafar Husain .	ظفر حسين	Zaríf . .	ظريف
Záhid . .	زاهد	Ziyárat . .	زيارت
Zaid 'Ali .	زيد علي	Zuhúr Muhammad . .	ظهور محمد
Zaid Gul. .	زيد گل	Zuhúrullah .	ظهورالله
Zamán . .	زمان	Zul-fiḳár . .	ذوالفقار
Zamán 'Ali .	زمان علي	Zul-fiḳár 'Ali .	ذوالفقار علي
Zámin Sháh .	ضامن شاه		